JAMES M^CNAIR'S VEGETARIAN PIZZA

Photography and Styling by James McNair

Chronicle Books • San Francisco

Printed in Hong Kong.

Library of Congress
Cataloging-in-Publication Data
Available

ISBN: 0-8118-0109-8.
ISBN: 0-8118-0100-4 (pbk.)

Distributed in Canada by
Raincoast Books
112 East Third Avenue
Vancouver, British Columbia V5T 1C8

10 9 8 7 6 5 4 3 2 1

Chronicle Books
275 Fifth Street
San Francisco, California 94103

For two great friends, Jan Ellis and Meri McEneny, who have been loving and supportive through the roller-coaster ride of recent years, and who helped reacquaint me with the glories of the vegetarian table.

Produced by The Rockpile Press, Lake Tahoe and the Napa Valley

Art direction, prop and food styling, and book design by James McNair

Editorial, styling, and photographic assistance by Andrew Moore

Typography and mechanical production by CTA Graphics

CONTENTS

INTRODUCTION

Although I'm not a vegetarian, I find myself eating more and more meatless main dishes, as well as meals that downplay the role of meat. And as my favorite pizza toppings have always been simple combinations such as garden-ripe tomatoes, fresh basil, and garlic with or without cheese, or grilled eggplant with sweet peppers, pizza ranks high on my list of vegetarian meal choices. Along with these changes in my eating habits, I've been happy to find that many upscale restaurants that offer pizza—as well as pizzerias everywhere—are including more meatless versions on their menus.

Pizza, minus high-fat toppings such as pepperoni and sausage, has been described by some nutritionists as a near-perfect food. Most of the pizzas in this book supply basic nutrients in almost the exact amounts recommended in the dietary goals outlined by the federal government: 15 percent protein, 27 percent fat, and 58 percent carbohydrate. When made with less oil and cheese or reduced-fat cheese, the fat percentage can drop even further.

To their great credit, the Italians invented pizza, but in recent years I think the humble pie has been gloriously enhanced by creative American chefs. Unlike the majority of Italian cooks whose national pride won't allow them to break with the traditions of classic toppings (which I admit are absolutely wonderful), in America the concept of pizza has been expanded to include flavors from around the globe. I was recently amused to read where a doyenne of traditional Italian cooking warned readers not to add goat's milk cheese to pizza because it doesn't taste authentically Italian. To my way of thinking, this tangy cheese, melting into a crisp, chewy crust, is a new hallmark of great pizza.

With their wide range of tastes and international flavorings, the vegetarian pizzas that follow will be so delicious and satisfying that even dedicated carnivores will not miss the meat.

USING THIS BOOK

If you are not familiar with the techniques described in *Pizza,* my first book on preparing this favorite food, please read the next several pages very carefully. Here you will learn, step by step, how to make successful pizzas and calzone.

Although the finished pies will be tastier when made with homemade crusts, many pizzas can be prepared with ready-to-use, quick-and-easy alternatives such as thawed frozen bread dough, take-out fresh pizza dough from a pizzeria, or the packaged prebaked crusts sold in many supermarkets. Middle Eastern pocket bread (pita), handmade thick corn tortillas, or even French bread may be substituted for the dough, crowned with toppings, and baked to create a tasty pizzalike dish.

My recipes suggest the number of servings that the crust and filling will make, but they leave you the option of making a single large pizza or dividing the dough into several individual-sized pies or a host of tiny *pizzette.* Of course, any fresh dough may be folded over the fillings and turned into calzone or their smaller counterparts, *calzonetti;* likewise, the recipes for calzone may be left unfolded and baked as flat pizzas.

The topping amounts are sufficient for covering the amount of fresh dough yielded by the recipe for Basic Pizza Dough (page 12) or for about two pounds of purchased fresh or thawed frozen dough. These topping amounts will also cover two large packaged prebaked Italian bread crusts (such as those made by Boboli) or four to six individual-sized prebaked crusts. Some people like only a light pizza topping, while others enjoy piling on the ingredients. Feel free to adjust my suggested proportions, which lean toward a heavy ratio of toppings to crust, to fit your own taste.

BASICS

Ingredients

YEASTS

Choose either active dry yeast or quick-rising dry yeast, which cuts the rising time of dough by about 20 percent. Whichever form of granulated yeast you choose, always check its expiration date before using. Read more about yeast in the Basic Pizza Dough recipe on page 12.

The well-worn admonition always to use the freshest and finest ingredients available holds especially true for vegetarian pizza. This is not the time to clean the refrigerator of vegetables that are past their prime. Choose vegetables that are immaculately fresh and packed with seasonal flavor. And don't skimp on the crust either.

Flours. For well-textured, extra-crispy crusts, choose bread flour or semolina flour. Bread flour, used by most pizzerias, is made from hard northern spring wheat. It has a high gluten content that raises yeast dough to its maximum volume, which results in a dough that can be stretched quite thinly. Semolina flour, the same type used in quality dried pasta, is milled from hard durum wheat. It requires the addition of a little more water to the dough than is necessary with bread flour or all-purpose flour. Dough made of semolina or bread flour takes longer to knead and rise than dough made with all-purpose flour, but the resulting crispy crusts make the extra effort and time worthwhile.

Although unbleached all-purpose flour is a blend of hard and soft wheats, its gluten content is high enough to make excellent crusts. It requires less moisture, kneading, and rising time than bread or semolina flour. If you use unbleached all-purpose flour, omit the second rising described in the Basic Pizza Dough recipe.

The amount of flour you'll end up kneading into the dough depends on the type of flour used, as already explained, and the amount of moisture in the air. When humidity is high, the dough will be sticky and you will need to add more flour. If the dough is too dry, you must add extra water; be sure to add it only a small bit at a time to prevent the dough from becoming too wet.

Oils. The addition of oil to pizza dough creates a crisp crust with a tender interior. I also usually brush it on the dough before cooking to keep the crust from drying out during baking and to insure a golden brown color. Plus, I like to swab the edges of the crust with oil as soon as the pizza comes out of the oven to add a little moisture and flavor.

For most pizzas, the oil of choice is olive oil. The nature of olive oil varies according to the method by which it was produced. I prefer the rich green color and fresh fruity flavor of extra-virgin olive oil. The finest olives are pressed by hand to produce this highest-quality olive oil, a process that also makes it the most expensive. Olive oil labeled simply "virgin" is made from the first pressing of olives of lesser quality; it is quite good, but less fruity tasting than extra-virgin oil. If you prefer a lighter-tasting olive oil, look for the golden color of "pure" olive oil, produced from the second or third pressing of the olives.

I use lightly flavored vegetable oil for greasing screens and pans and in recipes where olive oil would overwhelm or not be compatible with the toppings. You may also experiment with intensely flavored walnut oil, Asian sesame oil, and hot chile oil, all of which add unique character to vegetarian pizzas.

Cheeses. Contrary to the popular belief that pizza is always a cheese-and-tomato pie topped with other ingredients, you can make great pizzas without any cheese. Smooth-melting cheeses are, however, essential to the success of many pizzas, and mozzarella is the type used most often. Unfortunately, the majority of widely available factory-made mozzarella melts into a rubbery mass. Excellent alternatives include fresh mozzarella made by small cheese factories in many parts of the country or made daily by hand in large Italian communities throughout the United States. Although expensive, fresh mozzarella imported from Italy, especially the variety made from water buffalo's milk, melts into a wonderful pizza topping. If you locate fresh cheeses packed in liquid but can not use them the same day, store them up to a couple of days immersed in a solution of water mixed with a little skimmed milk; change the solution daily. Rinse the fresh mozzarella before slicing or shredding it.

SAUCES

Please forget about canned pizza sauces. When a recipe calls for tomato sauce—although most of mine don't— make your own simple version from flavorful ripe or canned tomatoes or use my recipe on page 92. In this book you'll discover some surprising sauces, from Chinese hoisin to southwestern-style salsa, that add new dimensions to pizza.

When sauce is added to a pizza, reverse the common pizzeria order of ingredients. Put a layer of cheese or another ingredient atop the dough before adding sauce; the cheese seals the crust and prevents it from getting soggy, which is what can happen when the sauce comes in direct contact with the dough.

If you don't have access to fresh or high-quality mozzarella, here are a few tips to prevent commercial cheese from becoming rubbery. Shred or chop the cheese instead of slicing it; it will melt more smoothly. Shredded factory-made mozzarella may be tossed in olive oil and set aside to soften for about an hour before cooking to approximate the creaminess of its Italian counterpart. Blending mozzarella with other good-melting cheeses also results in a creamy melt. I routinely mix mozzarella with Italian Fontina or provolone, Dutch Gouda, French Gruyère, Vermont Cheddar, California Monterey jack, or any other cheese that melts nicely. Often I forget the mozzarella and use these and other cheeses in combination or alone. If you choose quickly melting soft cheeses such as triple crème, Brie, or cream cheese, partially bake the crust before adding the cheese. Be adventuresome and try your favorites; chances are they'll work.

I often finish off a fresh-from-the-oven pizza with Parmesan cheese. If you don't go with top-of-the-line Parmigiano-Reggiano, which is costly but definitely worth it, choose the best similar grating cheese you can find. Italy protects the real thing with restricted labeling; similar Italian cheeses must be tagged *grana*. Some cheeses produced outside of Italy are labeled Parmesan, but bear little resemblance to the classic. Others, such as Asiago or a few domestic "Parmesans," are decent substitutes.

In my recipes, I've suggested an amount of cheese, but since some of us like only a sprinkling and others of us enjoy a lot, adjust the quantity to taste. If you do not eat dairy products, omit the cheese.

Tomatoes. You may be surprised to discover that neither tomatoes nor tomato sauce are called for in the majority of recipes in this book. As with cheese, they are not *di rigore* for first-rate pizza. When tomatoes are called for, be sure to choose vine-ripened fruits with plenty of flavor. Most fresh tomatoes sold in supermarkets have been developed for shipping and long storage, resulting in tasteless fruits. When you can't find good-tasting tomatoes, keep in mind that cherry tomatoes usually have good flavor. In recipes where fresh tomatoes are not the primary topping, it is better to use canned Italian plum tomatoes rather than insipid fresh ones.

Equipment

Pizza crusts are crispiest when baked directly on preheated unglazed quarry tiles, commercial baking stones, or pizza screens that allow direct contact with hot, dry heat.

The single most important piece of pizza baking equipment in my kitchen is the pizza screen, a round of heavy-gauge wire mesh bordered with strong wire tape. Since discovering pizza screens, which are made for professional pizzerias and sold in restaurant equipment outlets and well-stocked kitchenware stores, I rarely bother with lining my oven floor with quarry tiles or baking on pizza stones (which are usually too small to be effective). A screen is far easier to use than assembling a pizza on a wooden peel, the flat paddle-shaped spatula made for transferring pizzas directly onto a preheated stone surface. Screen-baked pizzas have a wonderfully crisp crust, although it may be even slightly crisper if you place the screen directly on preheated tiles or a stone.

For baking flat pizzas or calzone directly on a piping-hot baking surface, line an oven with unglazed quarry tiles (available from flooring supply houses or building supply stores) or insert a baking stone. In a gas oven, position the tiles or stone directly on the oven floor. In an electric stove, arrange the tiles or stone on the lowest rack of the oven. When using tiles, leave a one-inch clearance between the tiles and the oven walls for air circulation and avoid covering any vents that may be in the oven floor. For baking on a pizza screen or a vented flat pan without the use of tiles or a stone, position an oven rack at the highest position.

If you cannot locate pizza screens or do not wish to bake directly on hot tiles, purchase a flat pizza pan with ventilation holes that allow direct heat to reach the bottom of the crust. Old-fashioned pizza pans without such holes should be avoided, as the crust gets too greasy and/or soggy when trapped inside a pan. An exception to this rule is deep-dish pizzas, which must be baked in pans with high sides; I prefer springform pans for easy removal of deep-dish pies.

For information on other pizza-baking equipment, please see my book *Pizza*.

EASY MIXING

For quick-and-easy pizza crusts, I cannot overemphasize the importance of a *heavy-duty standing electric mixer* with a dough hook attachment. In only 10 minutes, the dough can be mixed and kneaded.

If you knead dough by hand, a *dough scraper* is essential. This wooden-handled utensil has a flexible metal blade for prying up sticky dough from work surfaces.

Basic Pizza Dough

1 tablespoon granulated sugar
1 cup warm (110° to 115° F.) water
1 envelope (¼ ounce) active dry yeast
3¼ cups bread, semolina, or
    unbleached all-purpose flour, or
    a combination
1 teaspoon salt
¼ cup olive oil, preferably
    extra-virgin

This detailed recipe is the most important part of this book, and I encourage you to read it through several times before starting to bake a pizza. Only then will you understand the steps necessary for creating all sizes and types of pizza. Once you grasp fully the various elements—mixing, kneading, shaping, cooking—of pizza making, the process will become clear and quite easy. With just a little practice, you will be quickly turning out the most scrumptious pizzas you've ever tasted and creating your own countless variations.

Any type of pizza can be made with this basic dough. Alter the taste and texture of the crust by using one of the flavorful variations in the sidebar on the opposite page. The recipe can be doubled if you're entertaining a crowd or just want to prepare extra dough for freezing.

In a small bowl, dissolve the sugar (which "feeds" the yeast) in the warm water. The water should register 110° to 115° F. on an instant-read thermometer. Alternatively, learn to judge the temperature by touch; the water should be warm to your finger but not too hot—the temperature of a comfortable bath. Water that is too hot will kill the yeast; water that is too cold will not activate it. Sprinkle the yeast over the water and stir gently until it dissolves, about 1 minute. When the yeast is mixed with the water at the proper temperature, a smooth, beige mixture results. (If the yeast clumps together and the water stays clear, discard the mixture and start over.) Let stand in a warm spot until a thin layer of creamy foam covers the surface, about 5 minutes, indicating that the yeast is effective. (Discard the mixture and start over with a fresh package of yeast if bubbles have not formed within 5 minutes.)

Mixing.

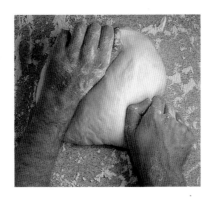

Kneading.

To mix and knead the dough by hand, combine 3 cups of the flour with the salt in a large mixing bowl. Make a well in the center of the flour and pour in the yeast mixture and the oil. Using a wooden spoon, vigorously stir the flour into the well, beginning in the center and working toward the sides of the bowl, until the flour is incorporated and the soft dough just begins to hold together.

Turn the dough out onto a lightly floured surface. Dust your hands with flour and knead the dough gently in the following manner: press down on the dough with the heels of your hands and push it away from you, then partially fold it back over itself. Shift it a quarter turn and repeat the procedure. While kneading, very gradually add just enough of the remaining ¼ cup flour until the dough is no longer sticky or tacky; this should take about 5 minutes. As you work, use a metal dough scraper to pry up any bits of dough that stick to the work surface. Continue kneading until the dough is smooth, elastic, and shiny, 10 to 15 minutes longer. Knead the dough only until it feels smooth and springy; too much kneading overdevelops the gluten in the flour and results in a tough crust.

PIZZA DOUGH VARIATIONS

To create crusts with a variety of flavors and textures, make the following changes to the recipe for Basic Pizza Dough.

CORNMEAL DOUGH. Substitute 1 cup yellow cornmeal or polenta (coarse cornmeal) for an equal amount of the flour. Stir the cornmeal, flour, and salt together before adding the yeast mixture.

CRACKED PEPPER DOUGH. Add about 3 tablespoons freshly cracked black pepper while kneading the dough.

CURRIED DOUGH. Add 2 tablespoons high-quality curry powder along with the salt.

FOCACCIA DOUGH. Increase the amount of salt to 2 teaspoons and the amount of water to 1½ cups. Omit the olive oil from the mixture, but generously brush the rolled-out dough with olive oil.

HERBED DOUGH. Add 3 tablespoons minced fresh herbs or 1 tablespoon crumbled dried herbs while kneading the dough.

SEEDED DOUGH. Add about ¼ cup sesame seeds, lightly toasted, or ¼ cup poppy seeds while kneading the dough.

SPICY DOUGH. Add 2 tablespoons ground paprika and 1 tablespoon ground cayenne pepper or other ground hot chile along with the salt.

SWEET DOUGH. Add ¼ cup granulated sugar with the flour and reduce the salt to ½ teaspoon. Use flavorless canola oil or other high-quality vegetable oil instead of olive oil.

WHOLE-WHEAT DOUGH. Substitute 1 cup whole-wheat flour for an equal amount of the white flour. Stir the flours and the salt together before adding the yeast mixture.

Rising.

To mix and knead the dough in a heavy-duty standing electric mixer, combine 3 cups of the flour, the salt, yeast mixture, and oil, if using, in the large mixer bowl. Attach the flat beater, gradually turn on the machine to the medium speed, and beat until well mixed, about 1 minute. Replace the flat beater with the dough hook and knead at medium speed until the dough is smooth and elastic, about 5 minutes. Pinch off a piece of dough and feel it. If it is sticky, continue kneading while gradually adding just enough of the remaining ¼ cup flour for the dough to lose its stickiness. If the dough is dry and crumbly, add warm water, a tablespoon at a time, until the dough is smooth and elastic.

To mix and knead the dough in a heavy-duty food processor, add 3 cups of the flour and the salt to the beaker fitted with either a metal blade or a dough hook. Turn the machine on to combine the ingredients, about 5 seconds. Add the yeast mixture and oil and process continuously until the dough forms a single ball or several masses on top of the blade, about 30 seconds. Pinch off a piece of dough and feel it. If it is sticky, continue processing while gradually adding just enough of the remaining ¼ cup flour for the dough to lose its stickiness. If the dough is dry and crumbly, add warm water, a tablespoon at a time, until the dough is smooth. Turn the dough out onto a lightly floured surface and knead by hand, as described on page 13, for about 2 minutes.

After mixing and kneading the dough by one of the above methods, shape the dough into a ball and place it in a well-oiled bowl, turning to coat completely on all sides with oil. (This oiling of the dough prevents a hard surface from forming that would inhibit rising.) Cover the bowl tightly with plastic wrap to prevent moisture loss, and set aside to rise in a draft-free warm place (75° to 89° F.—a hotter environment may kill the yeast) until doubled in bulk, about 45 minutes for quick-rising yeast or 1 to 1½ hours for regular yeast.

While the dough is rising, line an oven with unglazed quarry tiles, position a pizza stone, or adjust the oven racks as described on page 10. Preheat the prepared oven at 500° F. for about 1 hour before assembling pizza.

As soon as the dough has doubled in bulk, use your fist to punch it down to prevent overrising. Squeeze the dough into a ball, pressing out all the air bubbles. If you are using bread flour or semolina flour, turn the dough in an oiled bowl to coat once more, cover the bowl tightly with plastic wrap, and refrigerate it until the dough is puffy, from 35 minutes to 1 hour. Omit this step if using all-purpose flour.

If you cannot bake the pizza dough within 2 hours of its rising, punch the dough down again, turn it in an oiled bowl to coat once more, cover the bowl tightly with plastic wrap, and refrigerate. (The dough can be punched down a total of 4 times and kept refrigerated for up to 36 hours before the yeast is exhausted and the dough unusable.) Let chilled dough come to room temperature before proceeding.

To prepare the dough for shaping, pull the top of the dough and tuck all seams under the bottom to create a ball with a smooth top. To make a 15- to 16-inch pizza, keep the dough in a single ball. To make two 12-inch flat pizzas, two 10-inch calzone, two 9-inch deep-dish pizzas, or a double-crusted 10-inch stuffed flat pizza, divide the dough into 2 equal-sized smooth balls. To make a stuffed deep-dish pizza, divide the dough into 2 pieces, one twice as large as the other. To make individual 8-inch flat pizzas or calzone, divide the dough into 4 to 6 equal-sized portions. To make appetizer-sized *pizzette* or *calzonetti,* divide the dough into 12 to 18 equal-sized portions.

If you wish to freeze dough for later use, wrap the pieces tightly in plastic wrap or seal in airtight plastic containers and freeze for up to 4 months. Before using, thaw in the refrigerator for 1 or 2 days or for a few hours at room temperature.

Dividing.

Rolling.

Stretching.

Shape the dough into crusts by one of the following methods.

To shape flat pizzas or calzone with a rolling pin, place a ball of dough on a lightly floured surface and dust the top of the dough lightly with flour. Using the heels of your hands, press the dough into a circle or other desired shape, then roll it out with a lightly floured rolling pin until it is about ¼ inch thick, keeping the edges a little thicker than the center. While rolling the dough, pick it up and turn it over several times to stretch it. Continue to keep the outer edges thicker than the rest of the round and add a little flour to the surface of the dough whenever needed to keep it from sticking. Rest one hand near the edge of the dough round and use the other hand to push the dough against it to form a slight rim around the dough, working your way completely around the perimeter of the dough. Lay the dough round on a cornmeal-dusted pizza peel or a lightly oiled pizza screen. Fill and bake as quickly as possible. To form the top crust of a stuffed deep-dish pizza, use the rolling-pin method just described, rolling the dough circle to fit inside the pan; omit forming the rim.

To achieve a super-thin crust for a flat pizza or calzone by stretching, knead the dough for about 1 minute. Lightly flour the work surface. Shape the dough ball into a flat disk about 1 inch thick and lightly flour both sides. Starting from the center of the dough, press it out quickly with the heels of your hands, working around the dough to create the desired shape, usually a circle, until the dough is about ½ inch thick. Dust with flour whenever needed to prevent sticking. Stop stretching before you reach the outer edge of the dough, which will form the rim of the pizza.

Rest one hand on the surface of the dough. Lift up a portion of the dough with the other hand and pull it gently away from the center, stretching it as thinly as possible. Continue moving around the dough, stretching it until it reaches the desired shape and size and is between ⅛ and ¼ inch thick. If a hole forms, pinch it closed. (Be very careful when shaping the cornmeal or whole-wheat variations by this method, as those doughs tear easily.) Now, rest one hand near the edge of the dough and use the other hand to push the dough against it to form a slight rim, working your way completely around the perimeter of the dough.

Once the dough is shaped, sprinkle a pizza peel with cornmeal or lightly oil 1 or more pizza screens or vented pizza pans. Lay the dough on the cornmeal-dusted peel or oiled screen(s). Following the individual recipes, top or fill the dough as quickly as possible and bake immediately.

If using a pizza screen or vented pizza pan, place the screen or pan directly on the hot tiles or pizza stone. If you have not lined the oven with tiles or a stone, place the screen or pan on the top rack of the preheated oven to prevent the direct heat from burning the bottom of the crust. Bake the pizza until the crust is puffed and golden or as directed in individual recipes, usually about 10 minutes on tiles or a stone and about 15 minutes on an oven rack; a calzone may require a slightly longer baking time.

If using a pizza peel, before transferring the assembled pizza or calzone to the oven, give the peel a quick, short jerk to be sure the bottom of the crust has not stuck to it. Place the peel in the oven, holding the pizza over the stone or tiles, then quickly jerk the peel back 2 or 3 times, hopefully leaving the pizza centered on the cooking surface. (It takes a bit of practice, so don't be discouraged if you lose a few pizzas.) Bake the pizza until the crust is puffed and golden or as directed in individual recipes, usually about 10 minutes; a calzone may require a slightly longer baking time. Slide the peel underneath the crust and remove the pizza from the oven. Use a metal spatula to lift a portion of the crust, if necessary, in order to slip the peel underneath.

To bake and serve multiple pizzas or calzone, assemble and bake as many pies at one time as the oven will accommodate; several screens are easier to work with when baking several pies at once. Remove each pizza or calzone as soon as it is done. If you cannot serve it immediately, do not cover it with aluminum foil to keep it warm; the crust will get soggy if it is enclosed in foil. If you wish to serve several pizzas or calzone at one time, it is best to bake them up to 1 hour ahead and, just before serving, reheat each one briefly, 2 or 3 minutes, in a preheated 500° F. oven.

Brushing.

Topping.

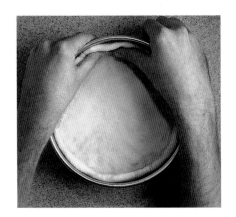

Lining deep-dish.

Stuffing deep-dish.

To shape and bake a deep-dish pizza, lightly brush a deep-dish pan with oil, place a ball of dough in the pan, and let it stand to soften for 10 minutes. Then flatten the dough with the heels of your hands and your fingertips to cover the bottom of the pan evenly. Pull the edge of the dough up the sides of the pan to form a 2-inch lip. Cover with plastic wrap and let the dough rise in the pan in a warm spot for about 20 minutes before filling and baking; for a thinner crust, fill and bake as quickly as possible, without further rising. Prick the dough every ½ inch with the tines of a fork and place on the bottom rack of the preheated oven for 4 minutes. Remove the crust from the oven, lightly brush with olive oil, and add the toppings. Return the pizza to the bottom rack of the oven for about 5 minutes, then move it to a rack in the upper portion of the oven and continue baking until the crust is golden and the filling is bubbly, about 20 minutes.

To shape and bake a stuffed deep-dish pizza, lightly brush a deep-dish pan. Reserve one third of the dough in the oiled pan and cover with plastic wrap. On a floured surface, roll out the larger portion of dough to fit the bottom and sides of the pan. Fit it into the prepared pan, pressing the dough gently onto the bottom and sides of the pan. Trim off the edge of the dough to form a 2-inch lip. Add the filling. Roll out the second piece of dough to fit just inside the pan, center it over the filling, and press the crusts together to seal. Cut a 1-inch slit in the top crust to allow steam to escape during cooking, then gently press the top crust down over the filling. Start the pizza on the lowest rack of the preheated oven for 10 minutes. Transfer the pan to a rack in the upper portion of the oven and continue baking until the crust is golden, about 20 minutes. When covering the top crust with a tomato or other sauce, some pizza bakers advocate spooning on the sauce before placing the pizza in the oven, although I prefer to add it during the final 10 minutes to avoid both overcooking the sauce and a soggy top crust.

To cut pizzas for serving, quickly jerk flat pizzas or calzone off the pizza peel or slide them off the wire screen onto a metal cutting tray or a flat cutting surface. Lift deep-dish pizzas from their pans onto the tray or cutting surface. Lightly brush the crust all over with oil. Using a rolling cutting wheel or a serrated bread knife, quickly and firmly cut all the way across the pizza in several places to form wedges; using a serrated knife, cut large calzone crosswise into thick slices. Serve sliced large pizzas or calzone directly from the cutting tray or transfer to a platter for passing. Slice small pizzas and serve on individual plates; leave individual-sized calzone whole. Serve all pizzas and calzone piping hot.

Makes enough dough for one 15- to 16-inch round flat pizza or deep-dish pizza; or two 12-inch round flat pizzas; or one double-crusted 10-inch round stuffed flat pizza; or two 9-inch round deep-dish pizzas; or one double-crusted 10-inch round stuffed deep-dish pizza; or two 10-inch folded calzone; or four to six 8-inch round individual pizzas; or twelve to eighteen 3-inch round appetizer-sized *pizzette* or *calzonetti*. Enough for 4 to 6 main-course servings, or 8 to 10 appetizer servings.

FRIED PIZZA OR CALZONE

For a change of pace, fry unadorned pizza dough or filled calzone until golden brown, keeping in mind that very little of the cooking fat is absorbed by the dough when the oil is heated to the proper temperature before dropping in the dough. You'll find that it is easier to handle the dough during frying when it has been formed into appetizer-sized *pizzette* or *calzonetti*.

In a deep-fat fryer, pour in olive oil, canola oil, or other high-quality vegetable oil to a depth of 2 inches and heat to 360° F. or until a small piece of bread turns golden within a few seconds. Carefully drop the pizza dough or filled, folded, and sealed calzone or *calzonetti* into the hot oil and cook, turning frequently, until golden, about 5 minutes. Using a slotted utensil, transfer to paper toweling to drain well.

Serve hot with a favorite tomato sauce, chile sauce, salsa, or other sauce and a sprinkling of cheese.

RECIPES

Tomato Garden Pizza

Do not despair if the variety of colorful tomatoes called for here is not available. As long as they are full-flavored and vine-ripened, red tomatoes alone will make a wonderful pizza. Just please don't make this pie with plastic-tasting supermarket tomatoes.

Prepare the Basic Pizza Dough, set it aside to rise, and preheat an oven to 500° F. as directed in the basic recipe. If using purchased dough or prebaked crust(s), set aside.

Brush a pizza screen or a ventilated pizza pan with vegetable oil or dust a pizza peel with cornmeal; set aside. On a floured surface, roll out the dough and shape it as directed in the basic recipe. Place the crust on the prepared screen, pan, or peel.

Brush the raw dough or the prebaked crusts all over with olive oil, then top with the cheese, leaving a ½-inch border around the edges. Distribute the tomatoes over the cheese, sprinkle with salt and pepper to taste, and drizzle evenly with olive oil.

Transfer the pie to the preheated oven and bake until the crust is crisp and the cheese and toppings are bubbly, about 8 minutes for prebaked crusts, or 10 to 15 minutes for fresh dough. Remove from the oven to a cutting tray or board and lightly brush the edges of the crust with olive oil. Garnish with the herb sprigs and flowers (if used). Slice and serve immediately.

Makes 4 to 6 main-course servings, or 8 to 10 appetizer servings.

Basic Pizza Dough (page 12), Herbed Variation preferably made with fresh basil, dill, or oregano, or about 2 pounds purchased dough, or 2 large or 4 to 6 individual-sized prebaked crusts
Vegetable oil for brushing, if using a pizza screen or pizza pan
Cornmeal for dusting, if using a pizza peel
Olive oil, preferably extra-virgin, for brushing crust and drizzling on top
3 cups freshly shredded high-quality mozzarella cheese (about 12 ounces)
3 pounds vine-ripened tomatoes, preferably red, orange, yellow, and green-striped varieties, peeled, if desired, and sliced
Salt
Freshly ground black pepper
Fresh herb sprigs, same type as used in dough, for garnish (optional)
Pesticide-free edible flowers such as nasturtiums for garnish (optional)

Garlic Pizza Chips

The idea for this appetizer came from Steamers, a lakeside cafe that specializes in pizza in King's Beach, California, where I've frequently enjoyed their version accompanied with frosty margaritas.

Prepare the Basic Pizza Dough, set it aside to rise, and preheat an oven to 500° F. as directed in the basic recipe. If using purchased dough, set aside.

In a bowl, toss the mozzarella cheese with the garlic and the 2 tablespoons olive oil. Set aside.

Brush a pizza screen or a ventilated pizza pan with vegetable oil or dust a pizza peel with cornmeal; set aside. On a floured surface, roll out the dough as thinly as possible and shape it as directed in the basic recipe. Place the crust on the prepared screen, pan, or peel.

Brush the dough all over with olive oil, then top with the garlic-mozzarella mixture, leaving a ½-inch border around the edges. Sprinkle with ½ cup of the Parmesan cheese.

Transfer the pie to the preheated oven and bake until the crust is crisp and the cheeses are bubbly, about 10 minutes. Remove from the oven to a cutting tray or board and lightly brush the edges of the crust with olive oil. Sprinkle with the remaining ½ cup Parmesan cheese. To serve as an appetizer, slice into numerous pieces about the size of corn chips and serve immediately.

Makes 4 to 6 main-course servings, or 8 to 10 appetizer servings.

VARIATION: Top the garlic-mozzarella mixture with sliced jalapeño chiles and/or tomato before sprinkling on the Parmesan.

Basic Pizza Dough (page 12), or about 2 pounds purchased dough
3 cups freshly shredded high-quality mozzarella cheese (about 12 ounces)
¼ cup minced or pressed garlic
2 tablespoons olive oil, preferably extra-virgin
Vegetable oil for brushing, if using a pizza screen or pizza pan
Cornmeal for dusting, if using a pizza peel
Olive oil, preferably extra-virgin, for brushing crust
1 cup freshly grated Parmesan cheese (about 4 ounces), preferably Parmigiano-Reggiano

Herbed Flat Bread with Roasted Garlic and Sun-Dried Tomato Cheese

Basic Pizza Dough (page 12), Herbed
    Variation made with rosemary or
    oregano

ROASTED GARLIC
4 whole garlic heads
2 tablespoons unsalted butter
Salt
¼ cup vegetable stock, preferably
    homemade
¼ cup dry red wine

SUN-DRIED TOMATO CHEESE
10 whole sun-dried tomatoes in olive oil
6 ounces creamy fresh goat's milk cheese,
    at room temperature
1 cup Yogurt Cheese (page 93) or
    8 ounces cream cheese, at room
    temperature
About 2 tablespoons oil from sun-dried
    tomatoes
Salt
Hot-pepper sauce such as Tabasco

Vegetable oil for brushing, if using a
    pizza screen or pizza pan
Cornmeal for dusting, if using a pizza peel
Olive oil, preferably extra-virgin, for
    brushing crust
Coarse salt
Fresh rosemary or oregano sprigs for
    garnish

Diners spread this piping-hot herb-scented crust with sweet roasted garlic scooped or squeezed from its papery shell and creamy tomato-cheese spread.

Prepare the Basic Pizza Dough and set it aside to rise.

To roast the garlic, preheat an oven to 350° F. Slice the garlic heads horizontally to cut away the top fourth of the cloves. Peel away the outer papery skin, leaving the garlic heads intact. Place in a small baking dish. Dot the cut surface with butter and then lightly sprinkle with salt. Pour the stock and wine into the pan, cover with aluminum foil, and bake until soft, about 1 hour, removing the foil occasionally to baste the garlic with the pan juices. Then remove the foil and bake for about 15 minutes longer. Remove from the oven and set aside at room temperature.

Increase the oven temperature to 500° F.

To make the tomato-cheese topping, combine the tomatoes, cheeses, oil, and salt and pepper sauce to taste in a food processor fitted with a metal blade or in a blender. Process until smooth. Pack into small crocks or bowls for serving and set aside at room temperature.

Brush a pizza screen or a ventilated pizza pan with vegetable oil or dust a pizza peel with cornmeal; set aside. On a floured surface, roll out the dough and shape it as directed in the basic recipe. Place the crust on the prepared screen, pan, or peel.

Prick the dough all over with a fork and brush it with olive oil. Sprinkle with coarse salt.

Transfer the dough to the preheated oven and bake until golden and crisp, 10 to 15 minutes. Check frequently and use the back of a wooden spoon to press down any areas that puff up. Remove from the oven to a cutting tray or board and lightly brush all over with olive oil. Garnish with the herb sprigs. Slice and serve immediately with the garlic and the tomato-cheese topping for spreading on the bread.

Makes 4 to 6 main-course servings, or 8 to 10 appetizer servings.

Antipasti Flat Bread

One gorgeous late-summer Sunday afternoon, I found myself happily seated around the family table of Arnie and Alma Tudal, who make some of the Napa Valley's finest Cabernet Sauvignon. I couldn't stop eating the warm *figassa* (a dialect term for *focaccia*) baked by Grandma May Cerruti, Alma's ninety-something mother. Most of us split the flat bread in half and stuffed it with flavorful antipasto ingredients, including salami for the carnivores, to eat out of hand.

When I asked for the recipe, I was intrigued to find that this chewy version of an old favorite uses ingredients in a ratio similar to that for my pizza crust. One difference is that no olive oil is used in the dough, although it is brushed generously on the bottom and sides of the pan and on top of the dough. Another difference is that Grandma May stirs everything together by hand, but I found that my electric mixer method was much easier and yielded similar results. Be sure that the dough rises longer than for pizza crusts.

Prepare the Basic Pizza Dough and set it aside to rise until tripled in bulk, about 3 hours. (Grandma May puts the dough in a closed oven with the light on for the first hour, then turns the light out for the remaining time.)

Preheat an oven to 375° F. and pour enough of the olive oil into a 9-by-13-inch pan to grease the bottom and sides generously.

Punch down the dough and place it in the center of the prepared pan. Using your fingertips, spread the dough to fit the bottom of the pan evenly; it will be springy and a bit difficult to spread. Generously brush the dough all over with olive oil. Bake until golden brown, 30 to 35 minutes.

Meanwhile, layer the tomato, pepper, and onion slices on a platter. Sprinkle to taste with salt and pepper, then drizzle with olive oil and vinegar to taste. Set aside. Place the artichoke hearts, pickled peppers, olives, and pickles in separate serving bowls. Set aside. Alternatively, arrange these ingredients on a serving platter and set aside.

Remove the bread from the oven to a cutting tray or board and brush the top with olive oil. Slice into small squares and serve immediately with the tomato salad, artichoke hearts, olives, and pickles alongside.

Makes 4 to 6 main-course servings, or 8 to 10 appetizer servings.

Basic Pizza Dough (page 12), Focaccia Variation
Olive oil, preferably extra-virgin, for brushing pan and dough and for marinating vegetables
Thinly sliced ripe tomato
Thinly sliced red sweet pepper
Thinly sliced red onion
Salt
Freshly ground black pepper
Red wine vinegar
Marinated artichoke hearts
Italian-style pickled peppers (*peperoncini*)
Assorted Italian-style olives
Assorted pickles

Salad Pizza

Basic Pizza Dough (page 12), preferably
  Whole-Wheat or Herbed Variation,
  or about 2 pounds purchased dough
Vegetable oil for brushing, if using a
  pizza screen or pizza pan
Cornmeal for dusting, if using a pizza peel
Olive oil, preferably extra-virgin, for
  brushing crust and drizzling on top
1 tablespoon minced or pressed garlic
3 cups freshly shredded high-quality
  mozzarella cheese (about 12 ounces)
1 cup freshly grated Parmesan cheese,
  (about 4 ounces), preferably
  Parmigiano-Reggiano

BALSAMIC VINAIGRETTE
2 tablespoons balsamic vinegar
1 teaspoon Dijon-style mustard
½ teaspoon sugar
About ¼ teaspoon salt
About ¼ teaspoon freshly ground black
  pepper
¼ cup fruity olive oil, preferably
  extra-virgin

4 cups small whole or torn tender salad
  greens, rinsed, dried, and chilled
½ small red onion, cut in half, then thinly
  sliced and separated into half rings
Pesticide-free edible flower petals such as
  nasturtiums or calendulas (optional)

The concept behind this creation, similar versions of which I've enjoyed at a couple of restaurants, is to top a hot cheese pizza with a mound of cool, crisp salad. The pie is then folded over and eaten as a sandwich. For variety, substitute any favorite cheese and salad dressing.

Prepare the Basic Pizza Dough, set it aside to rise, and preheat an oven to 500° F. as directed in the basic recipe. If using purchased dough, set aside.

Brush a pizza screen or a ventilated pizza pan with vegetable oil or dust a pizza peel with cornmeal; set aside. Divide the dough into 2 equal portions. On a floured surface, roll out each portion and shape as directed in the basic recipe. Place the crusts on the prepared screens, pans, or peel.

Brush each dough round all over with olive oil, then sprinkle with the garlic and top with the mozzarella cheese, leaving a ½-inch border around the edges. Sprinkle with the Parmesan cheese and drizzle evenly with olive oil.

Transfer the pies to the preheated oven and bake until the crusts are crisp and the cheese is bubbly, 10 to 15 minutes.

Meanwhile, to make the vinaigrette, in a bowl or in a jar with a cover, combine the vinegar, mustard, sugar, and salt and pepper to taste. Whisk well or cover and shake to blend well. Add the olive oil and whisk or shake until emulsified. Alternatively, the ingredients may be mixed in a food processor or blender.

Just before the pizza is done, in a bowl, combine the salad greens, onion, and flower petals (if used). Pour on the vinaigrette to taste and toss well.

Remove the pizzas from the oven to a cutting tray or board and lightly brush the edges of the crusts with olive oil. Mound the salad on the pizzas and serve immediately. At the table, slice each pizza in half. Instruct diners to fold each half together around the salad and eat out of hand like a sandwich.

Makes 4 main-course servings.

Chutney and Cheese Pizza

Basic Pizza Dough (page 12), Curried
    Variation, or about 2 pounds
    purchased dough, or 2 large or 4 to 6
    individual-sized prebaked crusts
Vegetable oil for brushing, if using a
    pizza screen or pizza pan
Cornmeal for dusting, if using a pizza peel
Canola oil or other high-quality vegetable
    oil for brushing crust
3 cups Yogurt Cheese (page 93) or
    24 ounces cream cheese, at room
    temperature
2 cups coarsely chopped fruit chutney
    (a favorite recipe or a high-quality
    commercial product)
About 3 tablespoons snipped fresh chives
    or minced green onion, including
    green portion

I've suggested a curry-flavored crust as a spicy counterpoint to the sweet chutney that melts into creamy cheese. If you use a plain crust or a commercial product, consider seasoning the cheese to taste with a good curry powder blend.

Prepare the Basic Pizza Dough, set it aside to rise, and preheat an oven to 500° F. as directed in the basic recipe. If using purchased dough or prebaked crusts, set aside.

Brush a pizza screen or a ventilated pizza pan with vegetable oil or dust a pizza peel with cornmeal; set aside. On a floured surface, roll out the dough and shape it as directed in the basic recipe. Place the crust on the prepared screen, pan, or peel.

Prick the raw dough all over with the tines of a fork and brush it or the prebaked crusts all over with canola oil or other vegetable oil. Transfer the crusts to the preheated oven and bake until the homemade crust begins to brown, 5 to 7 minutes, or until the prebaked crust is warm, about 4 minutes. Remove from the oven to a work surface.

Spread the partially baked or prebaked crusts with the cheese, leaving a ½-inch border around the edges, and spoon the chutney over the cheese. Return to the oven and bake until the cheese is hot but not completely melted, 4 to 5 minutes longer. Remove from the oven to a cutting tray or board and lightly brush the edges of the crust with canola oil or other vegetable oil. Sprinkle with the chives or green onion. Slice and serve immediately.

Makes 4 to 6 main-course servings, or 8 to 10 appetizer servings.

Potato-Leek Pizza

For the photograph, I divided the dough into a dozen equal portions and formed *pizzette* for serving as appetizers.

Prepare the Basic Pizza Dough and set it aside to rise as directed in the basic recipe. If using purchased dough or prebaked crusts, set aside.

Preheat an oven to 375° F.

Place the unpeeled potatoes in a roasting pan or other ovenproof shallow container. Add the garlic, the ¼ cup olive oil, about 1 tablespoon coarse salt, and about 2 teaspoons pepper. Turn the potatoes in the seasonings to coat all sides. Roast, stirring occasionally, until the potatoes are tender but not falling apart when pierced with a wooden skewer, about 35 minutes. Remove from the oven and set aside to cool. When cool enough to handle, slice crosswise about ¼ inch thick. Set aside.

Increase the oven temperature to 500° F.

In a sauté pan or skillet, heat the remaining 2 tablespoons olive oil over medium heat. Add the leek, 2 tablespoons of the fresh thyme or the 1 tablespoon dried thyme, and sauté until soft, about 5 minutes. Set aside.

Brush a pizza screen or a ventilated pizza pan with vegetable oil or dust a pizza peel with cornmeal; set aside. On a floured surface, roll out the dough and shape it as directed in the basic recipe. Place the crust on the prepared screen, pan, or peel.

Brush the raw dough or the prebaked crusts all over with olive oil, then top with the cheese, leaving a ½-inch border around the edges. Distribute the potato slices and leek evenly over the cheese, sprinkle with salt and pepper to taste, and drizzle evenly with olive oil.

Transfer the pie to the preheated oven and bake until the crust is crisp and the cheese and toppings are bubbly, about 8 minutes for prebaked crusts, or 10 to 15 minutes for fresh dough. Remove from the oven to a cutting tray or board and lightly brush the edges of the crust with olive oil. Sprinkle with the remaining 1 tablespoon fresh thyme (if used) and garnish with the garlic flowers (if used). Slice and serve immediately.

Makes 4 to 6 main-course servings, or 8 to 10 appetizer servings.

Basic Pizza Dough (page 12), preferably Cracked Pepper Variation, or about 2 pounds purchased dough, or 2 large or 4 to 6 individual-sized prebaked crusts
2 pounds small new potatoes, preferably an equal number each of purple-, red-, yellow-, and white-fleshed varieties
2 tablespoons coarsely chopped garlic
¼ cup plus about 2 tablespoons olive oil, preferably extra-virgin
Coarse salt
Freshly ground black pepper
2 cups thinly sliced leek, including pale green portion
3 tablespoons minced fresh thyme, or 1 tablespoon crumbled dried thyme
Vegetable oil for brushing, if using a pizza screen or pizza pan
Cornmeal for dusting, if using a pizza peel
Olive oil, preferably extra-virgin, for brushing crust and drizzling on top
3 cups freshly shredded aged Gouda cheese or Gruyère cheese (about 12 ounces)
Pesticide-free garlic blossoms for garnish (optional)

Tricolor Pepper Pizza

When late-summer bell peppers are sweet and plentiful, try this simple pizza. The peppers may be cooked together and sprinkled in a mélange over the crust or cooked separately and arranged in striking bands or concentric circles. If you cannot locate the French dried-herb mixture known as *herbes de Provence,* mix up your own blend by combining equal portions of dried crumbled bay leaves, basil, lavender, rosemary, summer savory, and thyme; sometimes a little dried orange zest and ground cloves are tossed into the mixture.

Prepare the Basic Pizza Dough, set it aside to rise, and preheat an oven to 500° F. as directed in the basic recipe. If using purchased dough or prebaked crusts, set aside.

In a sauté pan or heavy skillet, heat the ¼ cup olive oil over medium heat. Add the sweet peppers and onion and cook over low heat until the vegetables are quite tender and slightly caramelized, 35 to 45 minutes. Stir in the vinegar, garlic, *herbes de Provence,* and salt and pepper to taste and cook for 5 minutes longer. Remove from the heat and set aside.

Brush a pizza screen or a ventilated pizza pan with vegetable oil or dust a pizza peel with cornmeal; set aside. On a floured surface, roll out the dough and shape it as directed in the basic recipe. Place the crust on the prepared screen, pan, or peel.

Brush the raw dough or the prebaked crusts all over with olive oil, then spread with a thin layer of mustard and top with the cheese, leaving a ½-inch border around the edges. Distribute the pepper mixture over the cheese and sprinkle with the olives.

Transfer the pie to the preheated oven and bake until the crust is crisp and the cheese and toppings are bubbly, about 8 minutes for prebaked crusts, or 10 to 15 minutes for fresh dough. Remove from the oven to a cutting tray or board and lightly brush the edges of the crust with olive oil. Garnish with fresh herb sprigs (if used). Slice and serve immediately.

Makes 4 to 6 main-course servings, or 8 to 10 appetizer servings.

Basic Pizza Dough, preferably Herbed Variation made with *herbes de Provence,* or about 2 pounds purchased dough, or 2 large or 4 to 6 individual-sized prebaked crusts
¼ cup olive oil, preferably extra-virgin
2 yellow or golden sweet peppers, stems, membranes, and seeds removed, sliced into long, thin strips
2 red sweet peppers, stems, membranes, and seeds removed, sliced into long, thin strips
2 green sweet peppers, stems, membranes, and seeds removed, sliced into long, thin strips
2 cups thinly sliced yellow or red onion
2 tablespoons balsamic vinegar
2 tablespoons minced or pressed garlic
1 tablespoon dried *herbes de Provence,* or to taste
Salt
Freshly ground black pepper
Vegetable oil for brushing, if using a pizza screen or pizza pan
Cornmeal for dusting, if using a pizza peel
Olive oil, preferably extra-virgin, for brushing crust
Dijon-style mustard for spreading
4 cups freshly shredded Italian Fontina cheese (about 20 ounces)
About 1 cup pitted assorted oil-cured olives, preferably such Mediterranean varieties as Niçoise, Calabrese, and Kalamata
Fresh herb sprigs such as basil, lavender, or summer savory for garnish (optional)

Pepper, Leek, and Gorgonzola Pizza

Basic Pizza Dough (page 12), or about
    2 pounds purchased dough, or
    2 large or 4 to 6 individual-sized
    prebaked crusts
Vegetable oil for brushing, if using a
    pizza screen or pizza pan
Cornmeal for dusting, if using a pizza peel
Olive oil, preferably extra-virgin, for
    brushing crust and drizzling on top
3 cups crumbled Gorgonzola cheese
    (about 12 ounces)
2 red sweet peppers, roasted (page 93),
    stems, membranes, and seeds
    removed, and sliced lengthwise into
    strips about ⅓ inch wide
3 cups julienned leek, including pale green
    portion
Salt
Freshly ground black pepper
Canola oil or other high-quality vegetable
    oil for frying
About 2 tablespoons minced fresh parsley,
    preferably flat-leaf type (optional)

If you're cutting back on fats in your diet, omit the fried leek topping and use less cheese.

Prepare the Basic Pizza Dough, set it aside to rise, and preheat an oven to 500° F. as directed in the basic recipe. If using purchased dough or prebaked crusts, set aside.

Brush a pizza screen or a ventilated pizza pan with vegetable oil or dust a pizza peel with cornmeal; set aside. On a floured surface, roll out the dough and shape it as directed in the basic recipe. Place the crust on the prepared screen, pan, or peel.

Brush the raw dough or the prebaked crusts all over with olive oil, then top with the cheese, leaving a ½-inch border around the edges. Distribute the peppers and 1 cup of the leek over the cheese, sprinkle with salt and pepper to taste, and drizzle evenly with olive oil.

Transfer the pie to the preheated oven and bake until the crust is crisp and the cheese and toppings are bubbly, about 8 minutes for prebaked crusts, or 10 to 15 minutes for fresh dough.

Meanwhile, pour canola oil or other vegetable oil into a deep-fat fryer or deep saucepan to a depth of about 2 inches. Heat to 365° F, or until a small cube of bread turns lightly golden within a few seconds of being dropped into the oil. Add the remaining 2 cups leek and deep-fry, stirring frequently, until golden brown, 1 to 2 minutes. Using a slotted utensil, transfer the leek to paper toweling to drain.

Remove the pizza from the oven to a cutting tray or board and lightly brush the edges of the crust with olive oil. Sprinkle with the fried leek and minced parsley (if used). Slice and serve immediately.

Makes 4 to 6 main-course servings, or 8 to 10 appetizer servings.

Asparagus and Egg Pizza

Basic Pizza Dough (page 12), or about
1 pound purchased dough, or 1 large
prebaked crust
Vegetable oil for brushing, if using a
pizza screen or pizza pan
Cornmeal for dusting, if using a pizza peel
Olive oil, preferably extra-virgin, for
brushing crust and drizzling on top
1½ cups freshly shredded high-quality
mozzarella cheese (about 6 ounces)
1½ cups freshly shredded Cheddar cheese
(about 5 ounces)
6 eggs, at room temperature
Salt
Freshly ground black pepper
12 tender asparagus tips
¼ cup sunflower seeds, lightly toasted
(optional)
Shredded fresh basil leaves or minced
fresh chervil or tarragon for garnish
Fresh basil, chervil, or tarragon sprigs for
garnish (optional)

For this hearty breakfast or supper pizza, you'll need to make the crust a little thicker than usual. A packaged prebaked crust works well for this recipe.

Prepare the Basic Pizza Dough, set it aside to rise, and preheat an oven to 500° F. as directed in the basic recipe. If using purchased dough or prebaked crust, set aside.

Brush a pizza screen or a ventilated pizza pan with vegetable oil or dust a pizza peel with cornmeal; set aside. On a floured surface, roll out the dough in 1 piece and shape it as directed in the basic recipe; keep the dough about ½ inch thick. Prick the dough all over with a fork. Place the dough on the prepared screen, pan, or peel. Transfer the dough to the preheated oven and bake for 5 minutes; check frequently and use the back of a wooden spoon to press down any areas that puff up. Remove from the oven to a work surface. Reduce the oven temperature to 450° F. and position a rack in the top third of the oven.

Using your fingertips or a spoon, hollow out 6 indentations toward the outer area of the crust, leaving a thin unbroken shell of dough in the bottom of each hole. Brush the partially baked dough or the prebaked crust all over with olive oil. In a bowl, combine the two cheeses, then sprinkle them over the crust, leaving the hollows uncovered and leaving a ½-inch border around the edges. Break the eggs and carefully slip 1 egg into each hollow. Sprinkle the eggs with salt and pepper to taste. Arrange the asparagus over the cheese, sprinkle with the sunflower seeds (if used), and drizzle evenly with olive oil.

Transfer the pie to the oven rack and bake until the crust is crisp, the eggs are barely set, and the cheese and toppings are bubbly, 10 to 15 minutes; cover loosely with aluminum foil if the cheese and crust are getting too brown before the eggs are set. Remove from the oven to a cutting tray or board and lightly brush the edges of the crust with olive oil. Sprinkle with the shredded basil or minced chervil or tarragon. Garnish with the herb sprigs (if used). Slice and serve immediately.

Makes 6 main-course servings.

Corn and Tomato Pizza

This simple topping captures the flavors of summer.

Prepare the Basic Pizza Dough, set it aside to rise, and preheat an oven to 500° F. as directed in the basic recipe. If using purchased dough or prebaked crust(s), set aside.

In a bowl, stir together the tomato, corn, chopped savory or basil, and salt and peppers to taste.

Brush a pizza screen or a ventilated pizza pan with vegetable oil or dust a pizza peel with cornmeal; set aside. On a floured surface, roll out the dough and shape it as directed in the basic recipe. Place the crust on the prepared screen, pan, or peel.

Brush the raw dough or the prebaked crusts all over with olive oil, then spread with the mustard and top with the semisoft cheese, leaving a ½-inch border around the edges. Sprinkle with the grated hard cheese. Distribute the tomato-corn mixture over the cheese and drizzle evenly with olive oil.

Transfer the pie to the preheated oven and bake until the crust is crisp and the cheese and toppings are bubbly, about 8 minutes for prebaked crusts, or 10 to 15 minutes for fresh dough. Remove from the oven to a cutting tray or board and lightly brush the edges of the crust with olive oil. Garnish with the herb sprigs. Slice and serve immediately.

Makes 4 to 6 main-course servings, or 8 to 10 appetizer servings.

Basic Pizza Dough (page 12), Cornmeal Variation, or about 2 pounds purchased dough, or 2 large or 4 to 6 individual-sized prebaked crusts
3 cups peeled, seeded, chopped, and well-drained ripe tomato
2 cups fresh, drained canned, or thawed frozen corn kernels (from about 4 ears, if using fresh corn)
¼ cup chopped fresh summer savory or basil
Salt
Freshly ground black pepper
Ground cayenne pepper
Vegetable oil for brushing, if using a pizza screen or pizza pan
Cornmeal for dusting, if using a pizza peel
Olive oil, preferably extra-virgin, for brushing crust and drizzling on top
6 tablespoons Creole-style mustard or other flavorful mustard
2 cups freshly shredded mild semisoft cheese such as teleme or Bel Paese (about 10 ounces)
1½ cups freshly grated Pecorino Romano or Asiago cheese (about 6 ounces)
Fresh summer savory or basil sprigs for garnish

Roasted Chile and Goat's Milk Cheese Pizza with Avocado Salsa

When I want this pizza to capture even more of the flavors of the Southwest, I prepare the crust with blue cornmeal.

Prepare the Basic Pizza Dough, set it aside to rise, and preheat an oven to 500° F. as directed in the basic recipe. If using purchased dough or prebaked crusts, set aside.

Carefully rub off the blackened skin from the roasted chiles with your fingertips. Remove stems and scoop out seeds and membranes through the top. Set aside.

To make the Avocado Salsa, in a bowl, stir together all the ingredients except the avocado, including salt to taste. Cover and refrigerate for about 1 hour. (The salsa can be made up to this point and refrigerated for up to 6 hours.) Return to room temperature, then stir in the avocado just before serving.

In a bowl, mix together the cheeses; set aside.

Brush a pizza screen or a ventilated pizza pan with vegetable oil or dust a pizza peel with cornmeal; set aside. On a floured surface, roll out the dough and shape it as directed in the basic recipe. Place the crust on the prepared screen, pan, or peel.

Brush the raw dough or the prebaked crusts all over with olive oil, then sprinkle with the garlic and top with the cheese mixture, leaving a ½-inch border around the edges. Arrange the roasted chiles over the cheese, sprinkle with salt and pepper to taste, and drizzle evenly with olive oil.

Transfer the pie to the preheated oven and bake until the crust is crisp and the cheese and toppings are bubbly, about 8 minutes for prebaked crusts, or 10 to 15 minutes for fresh dough. Remove from the oven to a cutting tray or board and lightly brush the edges of the crust with olive oil. Scatter the Avocado Salsa over the pizza and garnish with cilantro and mint sprigs. Slice and serve immediately.

Makes 4 to 6 main-course servings, or 8 to 10 appetizer servings.

Basic Pizza Dough (page 12), Cornmeal Variation, or about 2 pounds purchased dough, or 2 large or 4 to 6 individual-sized prebaked crusts
10 fresh mild or hot red chiles such as New Mexico, roasted (page 93)

AVOCADO SALSA
1 cup fresh or thawed frozen yellow corn kernels, cooked in boiling water just until tender and drained
½ cup finely chopped red sweet pepper
⅓ cup finely chopped ripe tomato
2 tablespoons finely chopped red onion
1 tablespoon finely chopped fresh cilantro (coriander)
1 tablespoon finely chopped fresh mint
1 tablespoon minced fresh hot chile such as jalapeño or serrano, or to taste
2 tablespoons freshly squeezed lime or lemon juice
Salt
1 cup finely diced ripe avocado (cut just before serving)

2 cups crumbled fresh mild goat's milk cheese (about 10 ounces)
2 cups freshly shredded high-quality mozzarella cheese (about 12 ounces), preferably made from goat's milk
Vegetable oil for brushing, if using a pizza screen or pizza pan
Cornmeal for dusting, if using a pizza peel
Olive oil, preferably extra-virgin, for brushing crust and drizzling on top
2 tablespoons minced or pressed garlic
Salt
Freshly ground black pepper
Fresh cilantro and mint sprigs for garnish

Caribbean Jerk Cheese Pizza with Tropical Salsa

Basic Pizza Dough (page 12), or about
    2 pounds purchased dough, or
    2 large or 4 to 6 individual-sized
    prebaked crusts

TROPICAL SALSA
1 cup finely diced ripe mango
1 cup finely diced ripe pineapple
½ cup minced green onion
2 tablespoons minced fresh hot chile
½ cup minced fresh cilantro (coriander)
1 tablespoon rice vinegar or distilled
    white vinegar
Salt

JERK PASTE
½ cup coarsely chopped yellow onion
1 tablespoon coarsely chopped fresh hot
    chile, or to taste
¼ cup sliced green onion
1 teaspoon fresh thyme leaves, or
    ½ teaspoon crumbled dried thyme
½ teaspoon ground allspice
¼ teaspoon ground cinnamon
⅛ teaspoon freshly grated nutmeg
1 teaspoon salt
½ teaspoon freshly ground black pepper
Jamaican hot-pepper sauce (optional)

1½ cups freshly shredded high-quality
    mozzarella cheese (about 6 ounces)
2 cups freshly shredded white Cheddar
    cheese (about 6 ounces)
Vegetable oil for brushing, if using a
    pizza screen or pizza pan
Cornmeal for dusting, if using a pizza peel
Canola oil or other high-quality vegetable
    oil for brushing crust and drizzling
    on top
Pesticide-free edible flowers such as
    marigolds for garnish (optional)

In Jamaica, *jerk* is the term applied to a style of spicy grilled foods. It is also the name of the fiery paste rubbed on fish, meat, or poultry before cooking. Here I've used it to season the crust and cheese. The intense heat is tempered by a cooling fruit salsa strewn over the pizza the moment it comes out of the oven.

Prepare the Basic Pizza Dough, set it aside to rise, and preheat an oven to 500° F. as directed in the basic recipe. If using packaged dough or prebaked crusts, set aside.

To make the Tropical Salsa, in a small bowl, combine all the ingredients, including salt to taste. Cover and chill for at least 1 hour, then drain well and return almost to room temperature before using. (The salsa can also be made ahead of the dough and refrigerated for up to several hours.)

To make the Jerk Paste, combine all the ingredients in a blender or in a small food processor fitted with a metal blade, including hot-pepper sauce to taste, and run until smooth. Set aside.

In a bowl, mix together the cheeses; set aside.

Brush a pizza screen or a ventilated pizza pan with vegetable oil or dust a pizza peel with cornmeal; set aside. On a floured surface, roll out the dough and shape it as directed in the basic recipe. Place the crust on the prepared screen, pan, or peel.

Brush the raw dough or the prebaked crusts all over with canola oil or other vegetable oil, then spread with the Jerk Paste and top with the cheese mixture, leaving a ½-inch border around the edges. Drizzle evenly with canola oil or other vegetable oil.

Transfer the pie to the preheated oven and bake until the crust is crisp and the cheese is bubbly, about 8 minutes for prebaked crusts, or 10 to 15 minutes for fresh dough. Remove from the oven to a cutting tray or board and lightly brush the edges of the crust with canola oil or other vegetable oil. Spoon the Tropical Salsa over the pizza and garnish with flowers (if used). Slice and serve immediately.

Makes 4 to 6 main-course servings, or 8 to 10 appetizer servings.

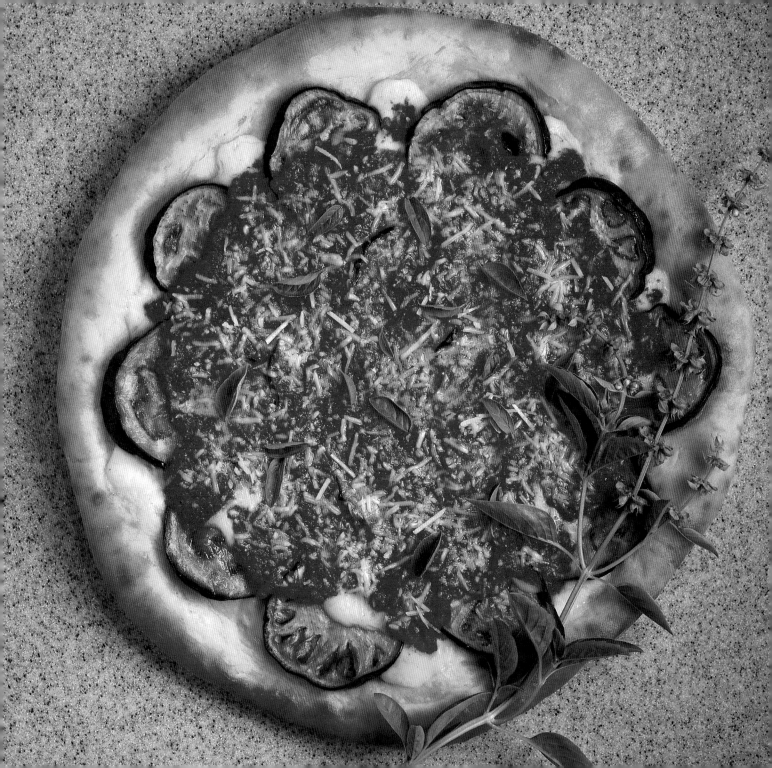

Eggplant Pizza, Parma Style

In this lighter version of a venerable favorite, white sauce replaces higher calorie cheese. Be sure to use the finest Parmesan cheese available.

Prepare the Basic Pizza Dough, set it aside to rise, and preheat an oven to 500° F. as directed. If using purchased dough or prebaked crusts, set aside.

Sprinkle both sides of the eggplant slices with salt and place on paper toweling. Cover with more paper toweling and place a wooden board or heavy weight on top for 30 minutes to draw out moisture.

Meanwhile, to make the White Sauce, in a heavy saucepan, melt the butter over low heat. Add the flour, whisk briskly to blend until smooth, and cook, stirring about 2 minutes; do not brown. Add the milk all at once and whisk until very smooth. Season with salt and pepper to taste. Simmer, stirring frequently, until thickened to the consistency of a rich cheese sauce, 20 to 25 minutes. Pour the sauce into a bowl, cover with plastic wrap placed directly on the surface to prevent skin from forming, and set aside. Prepare the Tomato Sauce as directed. Set aside.

Rinse the eggplant slices and pat dry with paper toweling. Dredge lightly with flour. Pour equal portions olive oil and vegetable oil into a sauté pan or heavy skillet to a depth of 2 inches and heat over medium-high heat. Add as many of the eggplant slices as will fit comfortably without crowding the pan and brown on both sides. Continue to cook, turning several times, until tender, about 5 minutes. Using a slotted utensil or tongs, transfer the eggplant to paper toweling to drain, then season to taste with salt and pepper. Brown the remaining eggplant slices in the same manner, adding more oil as necessary to prevent sticking.

Brush a pizza screen or a ventilated pizza pan with vegetable oil or dust a pizza peel with cornmeal; set aside. On a floured surface, roll out the dough and shape it as directed in the basic recipe. Place the crust on the prepared screen, pan, or peel.

Brush the raw dough or the prebaked crusts all over with olive oil, then top with the eggplant slices, overlapping slightly and leaving a ½-inch border around the edges. Spoon the White Sauce over the eggplant, then top with the Tomato Sauce. Sprinkle with about ¾ cup of the cheese and drizzle evenly with olive oil.

Transfer the pie to the preheated oven and bake until the crust is crisp and the cheese and toppings are bubbly, about 8 minutes for prebaked crusts, or 10 to 15 minutes for fresh dough. Remove from the oven to a cutting tray or board and lightly brush the edges of the crust with olive oil. Sprinkle with the remaining cheese and the whole or minced herb leaves. Slice and serve immediately.

Makes 4 to 6 main-course servings, or 8 to 10 appetizer servings.

Basic Pizza Dough (page 12), or about
    2 pounds purchased dough, or
    2 large or 4 to 6 individual-sized
    prebaked crusts
2 pounds globe eggplants, peeled and
    sliced crosswise about ½ inch thick
Salt

WHITE SAUCE
3 tablespoons unsalted butter
3 tablespoons all-purpose flour
2 cups milk
1 teaspoon salt
¼ teaspoon freshly ground white pepper

Tomato Sauce (page 92)
All-purpose flour for dredging
Equal portions high-quality vegetable oil
    and olive oil for frying
Salt
Freshly ground black pepper
Vegetable oil for brushing, if using a
    pizza screen or pizza pan
Cornmeal for dusting, if using a pizza peel
Olive oil, preferably extra-virgin, for
    brushing crust and drizzling on top
1 cup freshly grated Parmesan cheese
    (about 4 ounces), preferably
    Parmigiano-Reggiano
About 30 small whole fresh basil leaves,
    or 3 tablespoons minced fresh basil
    or oregano

Balsamic Onion, Japanese Eggplant, and Pesto Pizza

Basic Pizza Dough (page 12), or about
    2 pounds purchased dough, or
    2 large or 4 to 6 individual-sized
    prebaked crusts
2 tablespoons fruity olive oil, preferably
    extra-virgin
2 tablespoons unsalted butter
2 quarts thinly sliced red onion (about
    2½ pounds unpeeled)
2 tablespoons minced or pressed garlic
Salt
Freshly ground black pepper
¼ cup full-bodied red wine
¼ cup balsamic vinegar
2 tablespoons well-drained capers
Vegetable oil for brushing, if using a
    pizza screen or pizza pan
Cornmeal for dusting, if using a pizza peel
Olive oil, preferably extra-virgin, for
    brushing crust and drizzling on top
4 cups freshly shredded high-quality
    mozzarella cheese (about 1 pound)
6 slender Japanese eggplants, blossom
    ends discarded, sliced lengthwise into
    ¼-inch thick slices, brushed with
    olive oil and grilled, broiled, or baked
    until lightly browned and tender
Fresh Basil Pesto (page 92, or use a
    favorite recipe)
Minced red and golden sweet pepper for
    garnish

To top this pizza I chose ingredients similar to those used in an intensely flavored appetizer served at Showley's at Miramonte, one of my favorite restaurants in the Napa Valley.

Prepare the Basic Pizza Dough, set it aside to rise, and "reheat an oven to 500° F. as directed in the basic recipe. If using purchased dough or prebaked crusts, set aside.

In a large sauté pan or heavy skillet, combine the 2 tablespoons oil and the butter over medium heat. When the butter melts, add the onions and toss well to coat with the butter-oil mixture. Cover, reduce the heat to medium-low, and cook, stirring occasionally, until the onions just begin to color, about 30 minutes.

Remove the cover, add the garlic, increase the heat to medium, and season to taste with salt and a generous amount of pepper. Cook, stirring occasionally, until the onions are almost caramelized, about 25 minutes. Increase the heat to medium-high, add the wine and vinegar, and cook until the liquids evaporate. Stir in the capers and set aside.

Brush a pizza screen or a ventilated pizza pan with vegetable oil or dust a pizza peel with cornmeal; set aside. On a floured surface, roll out the dough and shape it as directed in the basic recipe. Place the crust on the prepared screen, pan, or peel.

Brush the raw dough or the prebaked crusts all over with olive oil, then top with the cheese, leaving a ½-inch border around the edges. Distribute the onion mixture over the cheese, arrange the eggplant slices on top of the onion mixture, and drizzle evenly with olive oil.

Transfer the pie to the preheated oven and bake until the crust is crisp and the cheese and toppings are bubbly, about 8 minutes for prebaked crusts, or 10 to 15 minutes for fresh dough. Remove from the oven to a cutting tray or board and lightly brush the edges of the crust with olive oil. Spoon pesto to taste over the eggplant and sprinkle the minced pepper over the pizza. Slice and serve immediately.

Makes 4 to 6 main-course servings, or 8 to 10 appetizer servings.

Sichuan Eggplant Pizza

Classic Chinese eggplant in garlic sauce is one of my favorite vegetable dishes. It also makes a marvelous-tasting pizza.

Prepare the Basic Pizza Dough, set it aside to rise, and preheat an oven to 500° F. as directed in the basic recipe. If using purchased dough or prebaked crusts, set aside.

If using slender Asian eggplants, discard blossom ends and cut the eggplants crosswise into slices about ½ inch thick; if using large globe-type eggplants, peel before slicing and then cut slices into bite-sized pieces. Place the cut eggplant in a bowl and add iced water to cover. Let stand for about 1 hour. Drain well and pat eggplant pieces dry with paper toweling.

In a small bowl, stir together the soy sauce, water, sugar, vinegar, and cornstarch; set aside.

In a wok, sauté pan, or skillet, heat the ⅓ cup canola oil or other vegetable oil over medium heat until almost smoking. Add the eggplant and toss until well coated with oil. Cover and cook for 2 minutes. Uncover and add the garlic and dried chile or chile paste or sauce and stir-fry until the eggplant is very tender, about 20 minutes. Stir the reserved soy sauce mixture to recombine, then stir it into the eggplant. Add the green onion and stir-fry until the sauce thickens, about 1 minute. Remove from the heat.

Brush a pizza screen or a ventilated pizza pan with vegetable oil or dust a pizza peel with cornmeal; set aside. On a floured surface, roll out the dough and shape it as directed in the basic recipe. Place the crust on the prepared screen, pan, or peel.

Brush the raw dough or the prebaked crusts all over with canola oil or other vegetable oil, then top with the cheese, leaving a ½-inch border around the edges. Distribute the eggplant over the cheese.

Transfer the pie to the preheated oven and bake until the crust is crisp and the cheese and toppings are bubbly, about 8 minutes for prebaked crusts, or 10 to 15 minutes for fresh dough. Remove from the oven to a cutting tray or board and lightly brush the edges of the crust with canola oil or other vegetable oil. Sprinkle with the chives or green onion. Slice and serve immediately.

Makes 4 to 6 main-course servings, or 8 to 10 appetizer servings.

Basic Pizza Dough (page 12), or about
  2 pounds purchased dough, or
  2 large or 4 to 6 individual-sized
  prebaked crusts
2 pounds eggplants, preferably slender
  Asian variety
Iced water for covering eggplant
½ cup soy sauce
½ cup water
2 tablespoons sugar
2 tablespoons rice vinegar
2 tablespoons cornstarch
⅓ cup canola oil or other high-quality
  vegetable oil
¼ cup chopped garlic
2 teaspoons crushed dried chile or Asian
  chile paste or sauce
½ cup sliced green onion, including green
  portion
Vegetable oil for brushing, if using a
  pizza screen or pizza pan
Cornmeal, if using a pizza peel
Canola oil or other high-quality vegetable
  oil for brushing crust
3 cups freshly shredded high-quality
  mozzarella cheese (about 12 ounces)
Snipped fresh garlic chives or slivered
  green onion tops

Olive Paste Pizza

Basic Pizza Dough (page 12), or about
  2 pounds purchased dough, or
  2 large or 4 to 6 individual-sized
  prebaked crusts
1 cup pitted imported ripe olives such as
  Niçoise
½ cup firmly packed fresh basil leaves
3 tablespoons capers, rinsed and well-
  drained
2 tablespoons coarsely chopped garlic
¼ cup olive oil, preferably extra-virgin
About 2 tablespoons freshly squeezed
  lemon juice
Salt
About ½ teaspoon freshly ground black
  pepper
Vegetable oil for brushing, if using a
  pizza screen or pizza pan
Cornmeal for dusting, if using a pizza peel
Olive oil, preferably extra-virgin, for
  brushing crust and drizzling on top
4 cups freshly shredded semisoft cheese
  such as Morbier, Port-du-Salut, or
  Taleggio (about 20 ounces)
2 cups chopped, peeled, and well-drained
  ripe tomato
1 cup sliced red onion, separated into half
  rings
Shredded fresh basil for garnish
Finely diced fresh red or golden sweet
  peppers for garnish

Tapénade, found throughout Provence, is an intensely flavored purée of olives. For this vegetarian pizza, I've eliminated the anchovies that are a traditional element in the mixture.

Prepare the Basic Pizza Dough, set it aside to rise, and preheat an oven to 500° F. as directed in the basic recipe. If using purchased dough or prebaked crusts, set aside.

In a food processor fitted with the metal blade or in a blender, combine the olives, basil leaves, capers, garlic, and the ¼ cup olive oil. Purée until smooth. Season to taste with lemon juice, salt, and pepper and blend well. Set aside.

Brush a pizza screen or a ventilated pizza pan with vegetable oil or dust a pizza peel with cornmeal; set aside. On a floured surface, roll out the dough and shape it as directed in the basic recipe. Place the crust on the prepared screen, pan, or peel.

Brush the raw dough or the prebaked crusts all over with olive oil, then spread with the olive paste, leaving a ½-inch border around the edges. Distribute the cheese over the olive paste, top with the tomato and onion, and drizzle evenly with olive oil.

Transfer the pie to the preheated oven and bake until the crust is crisp and the cheese is bubbly, about 8 minutes for prebaked crusts, or 10 to 15 minutes for fresh dough. Remove from the oven to a cutting tray or board and lightly brush the edges of the crust with olive oil. Sprinkle with the shredded basil and diced peppers. Slice and serve immediately.

Makes 4 to 6 main-course servings, or 8 to 10 appetizer servings.

Roman-Style Spinach Pizza

Basic Pizza Dough (page 12), or about
  2 pounds purchased dough, or
  2 large or 4 to 6 individual-sized
  prebaked crusts
4 pounds spinach, tough stems discarded
2 tablespoons minced or pressed garlic
6 tablespoons golden raisins, soaked in
  warm water to cover until plumped,
  about 15 minutes, then well drained
6 tablespoons pine nuts
¼ cup unsalted butter, melted
Salt
Freshly ground black pepper
Vegetable oil for brushing, if using a
  pizza screen or pizza pan
Cornmeal for dusting, if using a pizza peel
Olive oil, preferably extra-virgin, for
  brushing crust
4 cups freshly shredded Italian Fontina
  cheese (about 20 ounces)

Since my first visit to Italy a couple of decades ago, I've made the traditional Roman spinach dish exotically accented with pine nuts and raisins. The ingredients of this classic dish make an interesting pizza topping.

Prepare the Basic Pizza Dough, set it aside to rise, and preheat an oven to 500° F. as directed in the basic recipe. If using purchased dough or prebaked crusts, set aside.

Wash the spinach well. Place the damp spinach in a sauté pan or heavy skillet and cook, stirring frequently, over high heat until the spinach wilts and turns bright green, about 5 minutes. Drain in a colander and squeeze out as much liquid as possible. Transfer the spinach to a bowl and add the garlic, raisins, pine nuts, melted butter, and salt and pepper to taste. Toss to blend and set aside.

Brush a pizza screen or a ventilated pizza pan with veg table oil or dust a pizza peel with cornmeal; set aside. On a floured surface, roll out the dough and shape it as directed in the basic recipe. Place the crust on the prepared screen, pan, or peel.

Brush the raw dough or the prebaked crusts all over with olive oil, then top with the cheese, leaving a ½-inch border around the edges. Distribute the spinach mixture over the cheese.

Transfer the pie to the preheated oven and bake until the crust is crisp and the cheese is bubbly, about 8 minutes for prebaked crusts, or 10 to 15 minutes for fresh dough. Remove from the oven to a cutting tray or board and lightly brush the edges of the crust with olive oil. Slice and serve immediately.

Makes 4 to 6 main-course servings, or 8 to 10 appetizer servings.

Nacho Grande Pizza

Although a prebaked flour crust can be used, I strongly recommend your making a crunchier cornmeal version. Offer the toppings at the table for diners to spoon atop each slice as desired. Don't forget the margaritas!

Prepare the Basic Pizza Dough, set it aside to rise, and preheat an oven to 500° F. as directed in the basic recipe. If using purchased dough or prebaked crusts, set aside.

Brush a pizza screen or a ventilated pizza pan with vegetable oil or dust a pizza peel with cornmeal; set aside. On a floured surface, roll out the dough and shape it as directed in the basic recipe. Place the crust on the prepared screen, pan, or peel.

Brush the raw dough or the prebaked crusts all over with canola oil or other vegetable oil, then top with the cheese, leaving a ½-inch border around the edges. Distribute the beans over the cheese and drizzle evenly with canola oil or other vegetable oil.

Transfer the pie to the preheated oven and bake until the crust is crisp and the cheese is bubbly, about 8 minutes for prebaked crusts, or 10 to 15 minutes for fresh dough. Remove from the oven to a cutting tray or board and lightly brush the edges of the crust with canola oil or other vegetable oil. Slice and serve immediately with the toppings alongside.

Makes 4 to 6 main-course servings, or 8 to 10 appetizer servings.

Basic Pizza Dough (page 12), Cornmeal Variation, or about 2 pounds purchased dough, or 2 large or 4 to 6 individual-sized prebaked crusts
Vegetable oil for brushing, if using a pizza screen or pizza pan
Cornmeal for dusting, if using a pizza peel
Canola oil or other high-quality vegetable oil for brushing crust and drizzling on top
4 cups freshly shredded hot-pepper Monterey jack cheese (about 12 ounces)
2 cups well-drained, cooked pinto beans

OPTIONAL TOPPINGS
Chopped fresh cilantro (coriander)
Sliced fresh or pickled jalapeños
Fresh Tomato Salsa (page 92, or use a favorite recipe or a high-quality commercial product)
Sour cream
Guacamole (use a favorite recipe)

Stir-fry Pizza

Use any combination of seasonal vegetables, but limit the mixture to no more than five different kinds with similar cooking times. For the photo, I combined baby corn, green beans, carrots, and summer squash.

Prepare the Basic Pizza Dough, set it aside to rise, and preheat an oven to 500° F. as directed in the basic recipe. If using purchased dough or prebaked crusts, set aside.

In a small bowl, stir together the soy sauce, oyster sauce (if used), wine, vinegar, and cornstarch; set aside.

In a wok, sauté pan, or skillet, heat the ¼ cup canola oil or other vegetable oil over medium-high heat until almost smoking. Add the garlic and ginger and stir-fry briefly, then add the vegetables and stir-fry the vegetables until crisp-tender, about 3 minutes. Stir in the green onion and chile oil or chiles. Stir the reserved soy sauce mixture to recombine, then stir it into the vegetable mixture. Stir-fry until the sauce thickens, about 1 minute. Remove from the heat and drain off and discard any excess liquid.

In a small bowl, stir together the catsup and hoisin sauce; set aside.

Brush a pizza screen or a ventilated pizza pan with vegetable oil or dust a pizza peel with cornmeal; set aside. On a floured surface, roll out the dough and shape it as directed in the basic recipe. Place the crust on the prepared screen, pan, or peel.

Brush the raw dough or the prebaked crusts all over with sesame oil or chile oil, then spread with the hoisin mixture, leaving a ½-inch border around the edges. Top with the drained stir-fried vegetables. Sprinkle with the cheese (if used).

Transfer the pie to the preheated oven and bake until the crust is crisp and the toppings are bubbly, about 8 minutes for prebaked crusts, or 10 to 15 minutes for fresh dough. Remove from the oven to a cutting tray or board and lightly brush the edges of the crust with sesame oil or chile oil. Sprinkle with the toasted sesame seeds. Slice and serve immediately.

Makes 4 to 6 main-course servings, or 8 to 10 appetizer servings.

Basic Pizza Dough (page 12), preferably Seeded Variation made with sesame seeds, or about 2 pounds purchased dough, or 2 large or 4 to 6 individual-sized prebaked crusts
2 tablespoons soy sauce
2 tablespoons oyster sauce (optional)
2 tablespoons dry Chinese wine (Shaoxing) or dry sherry
2 tablespoons rice vinegar
1 tablespoon cornstarch
¼ cup canola or other high-quality vegetable oil
2 tablespoons chopped garlic
2 tablespoons chopped fresh ginger
4 cups sliced mixed fresh vegetables (see recipe introduction)
½ cup sliced green onions, including green portion
About 2 teaspoons hot chile oil, or several tiny fresh or dried Asian hot chiles
½ cup catsup
2 teaspoons hoisin sauce
Vegetable oil for brushing, if using a pizza screen or pizza
Cornmeal, if using a pizza peel
Asian sesame oil or hot chile oil for brushing crust
½ cup freshly grated Parmesan cheese (about 2 ounces; optional)
About 2 tablespoons sesame seeds, lightly toasted

Herbed Summer Squash Pizza

Basic Pizza Dough (page 12), or about
    2 pounds purchased dough, or
    2 large or 4 to 6 individual-sized
    prebaked crusts
2 pounds summer squash such as
    crookneck, pattypan, or zucchini,
    one type or a combination
Salt
Olive oil, preferably extra-virgin, for
    brushing squash and crust and
    drizzling on top
2 tablespoons coarsely chopped garlic
Vegetable oil for brushing, if using a
    pizza screen or pizza pan
Cornmeal for dusting, if using a pizza peel
4 cups crumbled fresh goat's milk cheese
    or feta cheese (about 1 pound)
¼ cup minced fresh summer savory,
    marjoram, or oregano
Freshly minced or grated zest of 1 lemon,
    or more to taste

During the peak of the summer squash harvest, try this intriguing combination of young, tender squash and tangy goat's milk or feta cheese.

Prepare the Basic Pizza Dough and set it aside to rise. If using purchased dough or prebaked crusts, set aside.

Cut the squash crosswise into slices about ¼ inch thick. Generously sprinkle each side with salt and place in a colander set over a bowl to drain for 30 minutes to eliminate excess moisture. Pat dry with paper toweling. (First rinse the slices under cold running water if you wish to rid them of the excess salt.)

Meanwhile, preheat an oven to 350° F.

Brush the squash slices on both sides with olive oil and arrange on a baking sheet. Sprinkle the slices with the garlic. Place in the oven and bake until tender, about 20 minutes. Remove from the oven and set aside.

Increase the oven temperature to 500° F.

Brush a pizza screen or a ventilated pizza pan with vegetable oil or dust a pizza peel with cornmeal; set aside. On a floured surface, roll out the dough and shape it as directed in the basic recipe. Place the crust on the prepared screen, pan, or peel.

Brush the raw dough or the prebaked crusts all over with olive oil, then top with the cheese, leaving a ½-inch border around the edges. Distribute the squash slices over the cheese, sprinkle with about 2 tablespoons of the minced herb, and drizzle evenly with olive oil.

Transfer the pie to the preheated oven and bake until the crust is crisp and the cheese is bubbly, about 8 minutes for prebaked crusts, or 10 to 15 minutes for fresh dough. Remove from the oven to a cutting tray or board and lightly brush the edges of the crust with olive oil. Sprinkle with the remaining minced herb and the lemon zest. Slice and serve immediately.

Makes 4 to 6 main-course servings, or 8 to 10 appetizer servings.

Spiced Pumpkin Pizza

When selecting pumpkin for cooking, avoid the rather flavorless type sold mostly for Halloween carving. Instead select such flavorful varieties as 'New England Pie,' 'Small Sugar,' or 'Triple Treat.' Or choose other flavorful winter squash such as 'Buttercup,' 'Delicata,' or 'Sweet Dumpling.'

Prepare the Basic Pizza Dough, set it aside to rise, and preheat an oven to 500° F. as directed in the basic recipe. If using purchased dough or prebaked crusts, set aside.

In a sauté pan or heavy skillet, combine the butter and vegetable oil over medium-low heat. When the butter melts, add the pumpkin slices and cook, turning occasionally, until the slices are lightly browned and tender but still hold their shape, 10 to 15 minutes; add a little additional butter and/or oil if the pumpkin begins to stick. About halfway during cooking, sprinkle with cinnamon, allspice, cloves, and salt and pepper to taste. Using tongs or a slotted utensil, remove the slices to paper toweling to drain briefly.

In a bowl, mix together the cheeses; set aside.

Brush a pizza screen or a ventilated pizza pan with vegetable oil or dust a pizza peel with cornmeal; set aside. On a floured surface, roll out the dough and shape it as directed in the basic recipe. Place the crust on the prepared screen, pan, or peel.

Brush the raw dough or the prebaked crusts all over with canola oil or other vegetable oil, then top with the cheeses, leaving a ½-inch border around the edges. Distribute the pumpkin slices over the cheese, sprinkle with the toasted pumpkin seeds (if used) and the crushed chile to taste, and drizzle evenly with canola oil or other vegetable oil.

Transfer the pie to the preheated oven and bake until the crust is crisp and the cheese and toppings are bubbly, about 8 minutes for prebaked crusts, or 10 to 15 minutes for fresh dough. Remove from the oven to a cutting tray or board and lightly brush the edges of the crust with canola oil or other vegetable oil. Garnish with cilantro. Slice and serve immediately.

Makes 4 to 6 main-course servings, or 8 to 10 appetizer servings.

Basic Pizza Dough (page 12), or about 2 pounds purchased dough, or 2 large or 4 to 6 individual-sized prebaked crusts
2 tablespoons unsalted butter, or as needed
2 tablespoons high-quality vegetable oil, or as needed
1½ pounds pumpkin or other winter squash (see recipe introduction), peeled, cleaned, and cut into uniform ½-inch-thick slices
1 teaspoon ground cinnamon
½ teaspoon ground allspice
¼ teaspoon ground cloves
Salt
Freshly ground black pepper
2 cups freshly shredded smoked Gouda cheese or other smoked cheese (about 8 ounces)
2 cups freshly shredded high-quality mozzarella cheese (about 8 ounces)
Vegetable oil for brushing, if using a pizza screen or pizza pan
Cornmeal for dusting, if using a pizza peel
Canola or other high-quality vegetable oil for brushing crust and drizzling on top
3 tablespoons hulled green pumpkin seeds, lightly toasted (optional)
Crushed dried hot chile
Fresh cilantro (coriander) leaves for garnish

Southern Stewed Okra Pizza

Basic Pizza Dough (page 12), Spicy
 Variation, or about 2 pounds
 purchased dough, or 2 large or 4 to 6
 individual-sized prebaked crusts
¼ cup (½ stick) unsalted butter
2 cups chopped yellow onion
1½ cups chopped red or green sweet
 pepper
2 pounds small okra, stemmed and sliced
 crosswise about ¾ inch thick
4 cups peeled, seeded, chopped, and well-
 drained ripe or canned Italian plum
 tomatoes
2 teaspoons red wine vinegar or balsamic
 vinegar
2 tablespoons minced fresh thyme, or
 1½ teaspoons crumbled dried thyme
1 teaspoon chile powder
½ teaspoon granulated sugar
About 1 tablespoon salt
About 1 teaspoon freshly ground black
 pepper
About 1 teaspoon ground cayenne pepper
2 cups freshly shredded high-quality
 mozzarella cheese (about 8 ounces)
2 cups freshly shredded white Cheddar
 cheese (about 6 ounces)
Vegetable oil for brushing, if using a
 pizza screen or pizza pan
Cornmeal for dusting, if using a pizza peel
Olive oil, preferably extra-virgin, for
 brushing crust
Fresh thyme sprigs for garnish (optional)

Every summer I crave the stewed okra from my Louisiana childhood. Strewn over a spicy crust, it makes a most unusual and satisfying pizza.

Prepare the Basic Pizza Dough, set it aside to rise, and preheat an oven to 500° F. as directed in the basic recipe. If using purchased dough or prebaked crusts, set aside.

In a sauté pan or heavy skillet, melt the butter over medium heat. Add the onion and sweet pepper and cook, stirring frequently, until the vegetables are soft but not brown, about 5 minutes. Add the okra and cook, stirring frequently, until tender, about 15 minutes. Add the tomatoes, vinegar, thyme, chile powder, sugar, and salt and ground peppers to taste. Cover, reduce the heat to low, and simmer, stirring occasionally, until the liquid evaporates and the mixture is fairy thick, about 30 minutes.

In a bowl, mix together the cheeses; set aside.

Brush a pizza screen or a ventilated pizza pan with vegetable oil or dust a pizza peel with cornmeal; set aside. On a floured surface, roll out the dough and shape it as directed in the basic recipe. Place the crust on the prepared screen, pan, or peel.

Brush the raw dough or the prebaked crusts all over with olive oil, then top with the cheeses, leaving a ½-inch border around the edges. Distribute the stewed okra over the cheese and drizzle evenly with olive oil.

Transfer the pie to the preheated oven and bake until the crust is crisp and the cheese and toppings are bubbly, about 8 minutes for prebaked crusts, or 10 to 15 minutes for fresh dough. Remove from the oven to a cutting tray or board and lightly brush the edges of the crust with olive oil. Garnish with thyme sprigs (if used). Slice and serve immediately.

Makes 4 to 6 main-course servings, or 8 to 10 appetizer servings.

White Vegetable Pizza
(Pizza Margherita Bianca)

Pizza Margherita bianca is an Italian classic topped only with mozzarella cheese. To give it an added vegetarian accent, crown the cheese with a mèlange of white vegetables such as garden-blanched asparagus, cauliflower, celery root (celeriac), endive, white corn, fennel, heart of palm, Napa cabbage, enoki mushrooms, peeled Jerusalem artichoke, leek (white portion only), white onion, parsnip, peeled potato, or white radish. Vegetables that would not become tender during the brief pizza baking time should be baked, steamed, or sautéed before assembling the pizza.

For the photograph, I topped each *pizzette* with a different white vegetable.

Prepare the Basic Pizza Dough, set it aside to rise, and preheat an oven to 500° F. as directed in the basic recipe. If using purchased dough or prebaked crusts, set aside.

Brush a pizza screen or a ventilated pizza pan with vegetable oil or dust a pizza peel with cornmeal; set aside. On a floured surface, roll out the dough and shape it as directed in the basic recipe. Place the crust on the prepared screen, pan, or peel.

Brush the raw dough or the prebaked crusts all over with olive oil, then top with the mozzarella cheese, leaving a ½-inch border around the edges. Distribute the vegetables over the cheese, season with salt and pepper to taste, sprinkle with about two thirds of the Parmesan cheese, and drizzle evenly with olive oil.

Transfer the pie to the preheated oven and bake until the crust is crisp and the cheese and toppings are bubbly, about 8 minutes for prebaked crusts, or 10 to 15 minutes for fresh dough. Remove from the oven to a cutting tray or board and lightly brush the edges of the crust with olive oil. Sprinkle with the remaining Parmesan cheese. Slice and serve immediately.

Makes 4 to 6 main-course servings, or 8 to 10 appetizer servings.

Basic Pizza Dough (page 12), or about
  2 pounds purchased dough, or
  2 large or 4 to 6 individual-sized
  prebaked crusts
Vegetable oil for brushing, if using a
  pizza screen or pizza pan
Cornmeal for dusting, if using a pizza peel
Olive oil, preferably extra-virgin, for
  brushing crust and drizzling on top
4 cups freshly shredded high-quality
  mozzarella cheese (about 1 pound)
4 cups chopped or sliced white vegetables
  (see recipe introduction)
Salt
Freshly ground white pepper
1 cup freshly grated Parmesan cheese
  (about 4 ounces), preferably
  Parmigiano-Reggiano

Athenian Pizza

Basic Pizza Dough (page 12), or about
    2 pounds purchased dough, or
    2 large or 4 to 6 individual-sized
    prebaked crusts
Vegetable oil for brushing, if using a
    pizza screen or pizza pan
Cornmeal for dusting, if using a pizza peel
Olive oil, preferably extra-virgin, for
    brushing crust and drizzling on top
3 cups crumbled feta cheese (about
    12 ounces)
1 red onion, thinly sliced and separated
    into rings
6 ounces fresh mushrooms, thinly sliced
1 cup pitted Kalamata olives
1 cup sliced pickled peppers *(peperoncini)*
3 tablespoons minced fresh oregano, or
    1 tablespoon crumbled dried oregano
Fresh oregano sprigs for garnish

This simple pizza combines some of the hallmarks of Greek cuisine: feta cheese, Kalamata olives, and oregano. If you wish, add some peeled, seeded, chopped, and well-drained fresh tomato along with the other toppings.

Prepare the Basic Pizza Dough, set it aside to rise, and preheat an oven to 500° F. as directed in the basic recipe. If using purchased dough or prebaked crusts, set aside.

Brush a pizza screen or a ventilated pizza pan with vegetable oil or dust a pizza peel with cornmeal; set aside. On a floured surface, roll out the dough and shape it as directed in the basic recipe. Place the crust on the prepared screen, pan, or peel.

Brush the raw dough or the prebaked crusts all over with olive oil, then top with the cheese, leaving a ½-inch border around the edges. Distribute the onion rings, mushrooms, olives, and peppers over the cheese, sprinkle with the oregano, and drizzle evenly with olive oil.

Transfer the pie to the preheated oven and bake until the crust is crisp and the cheese and toppings are bubbly, about 8 minutes for prebaked crusts, or 10 to 15 minutes for fresh dough. Remove from the oven to a cutting tray or board and lightly brush the edges of the crust with olive oil. Garnish with the oregano sprigs. Slice and serve immediately.

Makes 4 to 6 main-course servings, or 8 to 10 appetizer servings.

Black Bean Chili Calzone

1 cup dried black beans
¼ cup olive oil, preferably extra-virgin
½ cup chopped yellow onion
2 teaspoons chopped fresh or canned
    jalapeño or other hot chile, or to taste
1 teaspoon minced or pressed garlic
2 teaspoons minced fresh oregano, or
    1 teaspoon crumbled dried oregano
2 teaspoons minced fresh thyme, or
    1 teaspoon crumbled dried thyme
¾ teaspoon ground cumin
½ teaspoon ground coriander
2 bay leaves
3 cups vegetable stock, preferably
    homemade, or as needed
¼ cup tomato purée
Salt
Freshly ground black pepper
Ground cayenne pepper
Basic Pizza Dough (page 12), or about
    2 pounds purchased dough
4 cups freshly shredded white Cheddar or
    jack cheese (about 12 ounces),
    crumbled fresh goat's milk cheese
    (about 1 pound), or a combination
½ cup chopped fresh cilantro (coriander),
    or to taste
Vegetable oil for brushing, if using a
    pizza screen or pizza pan
Cornmeal for dusting, if using a pizza peel
Olive oil, preferably extra-virgin, for
    brushing crust
Minced fresh cilantro for sprinkling
Crushed dried hot chile for sprinking

This recipe can also be used for making a pizza: Layer the cheese and beans on a flat crust and sprinkle on the minced cilantro when the pie comes out of the oven.

Carefully pick over the beans to remove any shriveled beans and other impurities. Rinse well, place in a bowl, add cold water to cover, and let soak overnight. Drain and set aside.

In a soup pot or large, heavy saucepan, heat the ¼ cup olive oil over medium-high heat. Add the onion and chile and sauté until soft, about 5 minutes. Add the garlic, oregano, thyme, cumin, and coriander and sauté for 1 minute longer. Add the drained beans, bay leaves, and stock. Bring to a boil, then reduce the heat, cover, and simmer for 1½ hours.

Stir the tomato purée into the beans and season to taste with salt and black and cayenne peppers. Cover and simmer until the beans are tender, about 1 hour longer; add more liquid if necessary to keep beans covered during cooking.

Meanwhile, prepare the Basic Pizza Dough, set it aside to rise, and preheat an oven to 500° F. as directed in the basic recipe. If using purchased dough, set aside.

Drain the beans well to remove as much liquid as possible. In a bowl, toss the drained beans with the cheese and chopped cilantro. Set aside.

Brush 2 pizza screens or ventilated pizza pans with vegetable oil or dust a pizza peel with cornmeal; set aside. On a floured surface, roll out the dough and shape it into rounds for calzone as directed in the basic recipe.

Brush the raw dough all over with olive oil, then cover half of each dough circle with the bean-cheese mixture, leaving a ½-inch border around the edges. Fold the uncovered side over the filling and press the edges of the dough together to seal. Brush the dough all over with olive oil.

Place the calzone on the prepared screens, pans, or peel. Transfer to the preheated oven and bake until crisp and golden, about 15 minutes. Remove from the oven to a cutting tray or board and lightly brush the calzone all over with olive oil. Sprinkle with minced cilantro and crushed chile to taste. Serve immediately.

Makes 4 to 6 main-course servings, or 8 to 10 appetizer servings.

Mushroom and Brie Calzone

A rich blend of fresh wild mushrooms and creamy Brie makes a hearty filling for these savory pastry turnovers. Accompany them with a green salad for a complete meal.

Prepare the Basic Pizza Dough, set it aside to rise, and preheat an oven to 500° F. as directed in the basic recipe. If using purchased dough, set aside.

If desired, prepare the Red Chile Sauce. Set aside.

Slice or chop the mushrooms, discarding any tough stems.

In a sauté pan or heavy skillet, heat the 2 tablespoons olive oil over high heat. Add the mushrooms and onion and sauté for 1 minute. Add the butter, wine, and salt and pepper to taste. Continue sautéing until the vegetables are tender and the liquid evaporates completely, about 3 minutes. Stir in the marjoram or thyme. Remove from the heat and set aside.

Brush 2 pizza screens or ventilated pizza pans with vegetable oil or dust a pizza peel with cornmeal; set aside. On a floured surface, roll out the dough and shape it into rounds for calzone as directed in the basic recipe.

Brush the dough all over with olive oil. Using half of the cheese, divide it equally between the rounds and cover half of each dough circle with the cheese, leaving a ½-inch border around the edges. Drain off and discard any excess liquid from the mushrooms and divide them equally between the rounds, spreading them over the cheese. Top the mushrooms with the remaining cheese, dividing it equally. Fold the uncovered side over the filling and press the edges of the dough together to seal. Brush the dough all over with olive oil.

Place the calzone on the prepared screens, pans, or peel. Transfer to the preheated oven and bake until crisp and golden, about 15 minutes. Remove from the oven to a cutting tray or board and lightly brush the calzone with olive oil. If using the chile sauce, spoon a pool of the reheated sauce onto individual plates and top each with a serving of calzone. Garnish with the shredded greens. Serve immediately.

Makes 4 to 6 main-course servings, or 8 to 10 appetizer servings.

Basic Pizza Dough (page 12), or about
　　2 pounds purchased dough
Red Chile Sauce (page 93; optional)
1½ pounds fresh mushrooms, preferably
　　wild varieties such as chanterelles,
　　morels, porcini, or shiitakes
2 tablespoons olive oil, preferably extra-
　　virgin
1 cup chopped red onion
3 tablespoons unsalted butter
¾ cup dry white wine
Salt
Freshly ground black pepper
1 tablespoon minced fresh marjoram or
　　thyme, or 1 teaspoon crumbled dried
　　marjoram or thyme
Vegetable oil for brushing, if using a
　　pizza screen or pizza pan
Cornmeal for dusting, if using a pizza peel
Olive oil, preferably extra-virgin, for
　　brushing crust
1 pound Brie cheese (rind discarded), cut
　　into small pieces
Shredded cabbage or other crisp greens
　　for garnish

Curried Vegetable Deep-Dish Pizza

Use the filling and baking technique described here with other favorite fillings to create a variety of deep-dish pies.

Prepare the Basic Pizza Dough and set it aside to rise as directed in the basic recipe. If using purchased dough, set aside. Position a rack in the upper portion of an oven and another rack in the lower portion. Preheat the oven to 475° F.

In a sauté pan or heavy skillet, combine the butter and the 2 tablespoons vegetable oil over medium heat. When the butter melts, add the leek or onion and curry powder and cook, stirring frequently, until the leek or onion is soft but not brown, about 5 minutes. Stir in the coconut milk, increase the heat to high, and bring to a boil. Add the turnips or rutabagas, cover, reduce the heat to low, and simmer for 20 minutes. Stir in the carrots and cauliflower. Cover and simmer until the vegetables are tender, about 15 minutes longer. Stir in the peas, parsley, and lemon juice and salt to taste and simmer for about 3 minutes. Remove from the heat and drain off any excess liquid.

Lightly brush a 15-inch deep-dish pizza pan with canola oil or other vegetable oil. Press the dough into the pan (or divide it in half and press each half into an oiled 9-inch pan) as described in the basic recipe. Cover with plastic wrap and let the dough rise in a warm spot for about 20 minutes. Prick the bottom every ½ inch with the tines of a fork. Place on the bottom rack of the preheated oven for 4 minutes. Remove from the oven and lightly brush the crust with canola oil or other vegetable oil.

In a bowl, mix together the cheeses. Spread the cheese mixture completely over the bottom of the crust, then spoon the vegetable mixture over the cheese and drizzle lightly with oil. Place on the bottom rack of the oven for 5 minutes, then move to a rack in the upper portion of the oven and bake until the crust is golden brown and the filling is bubbly, about 20 minutes. Remove from the pan to a cutting tray or board and lightly brush the edges of the crust with canola oil or other vegetable oil. Sprinkle with the cashews, currants, green onion, and coconut. Slice and serve immediately. Offer the chutney at the table.

Makes 4 to 6 main-course servings, or 8 to 10 appetizer servings.

Basic Pizza Dough (page 12), Cornmeal Variation, or about 2 pounds purchased dough
3 tablespoons unsalted butter
2 tablespoons high-quality vegetable oil
2 cups chopped leek, including pale green portion, or yellow onion
2 tablespoons curry powder (to make your own, see my book *Stews & Casseroles* or use a high-quality commercial product)
2 cups homemade or unsweetened canned coconut milk
12 ounces rutabagas or turnips, peeled and cut into bite-sized pieces
12 ounces carrots, peeled and cut into bite-sized pieces
1 cup cauliflower florets (from about ½ small head)
1 cup shelled green peas (from about 1 pound unshelled)
¼ cup minced fresh parsley
About 3 tablespoons freshly squeezed lemon juice
Salt
Canola oil or other high-quality vegetable oil for brushing pan and crust and drizzling on top
2 cups freshly shredded high-quality mozzarella cheese (about 8 ounces)
2 cups well-drained high-quality ricotta cheese (about 1 pound)
¼ cup cashews, lightly toasted
3 tablespoons dried currants, soaked in hot water to cover until plumped, about 15 minutes, then drained
3 tablespoons minced green onion
3 tablespoons shredded fresh or dried coconut, lightly toasted
Fruit chutney (use a favorite recipe or a high-quality commercial product)

Vegetable-Stuffed Deep-Dish Pizza

Basic Pizza Dough (page 12), or about
 2 pounds purchased dough
Vegetable oil for brushing pan
Olive oil, preferably extra-virgin, for
 brushing crust
4 cups well-drained vegetable stew (see
 recipe introduction)
Tomato Sauce (page 92)
½ cup freshly grated Parmesan cheese
 (about 2 ounces), preferably
 Parmigiano-Reggiano
Fresh herb sprigs (same as those used in
 vegetable stew) for garnish

This double-crust pie may be filled with any favorite vegetable stew. See my book *Stews & Casseroles* for several possibilities, including Summer Garden Stew, Ratatouille Provençale, and Winter Vegetable Ragout. When preparing the vegetables for stewing, cut them into small pieces of uniform size.

Alternatively, the pizza may be filled with sautéed vegetables that are tossed with about 2 cups shredded good-melting cheese.

Prepare the Basic Pizza Dough and set it aside to rise as directed in the basic recipe. If using purchased dough, set aside. Position a rack in the upper portion of an oven and another rack in the lower portion. Preheat the oven to 475° F.

Brush a 12-inch deep-dish pizza pan with vegetable oil. Reserve one third of the dough in the oiled bowl and cover with plastic wrap. On a floured surface, roll out the larger portion into a 14-inch circle and fit it into the prepared pan, pressing the dough gently onto the bottom and sides of the pan. Trim off the edge of the dough to form a 2-inch lip. Fill the dough shell with the vegetable stew.

Roll out the reserved dough portion into a 12-inch circle. Place on top of the filling and press the crusts together to seal. Cut a 1-inch slit in the center of the top crust to allow steam to escape during baking, then gently press the top crust down over the filling. Brush the crust all over with olive oil.

Transfer the pie to the bottom rack of the oven and bake for 10 minutes, then move to a rack in the upper portion of the oven and bake for 10 minutes. Remove from the oven and spoon about 1 cup of the tomato sauce over the top. Sprinkle with the cheese. Return to the oven and bake until the crust is golden and the cheese is bubbly, about 10 minutes longer. Remove from the pan to a cutting tray or board. Garnish with herb sprigs. Slice and serve immediately.

Makes 4 to 6 main-course servings, or 8 to 10 appetizer servings.

Nut and Mascarpone Pizza

Inspired by the ingredients of a classic Italian pasta sauce, this nut-topped pizza makes a satisfying meal when accompanied with a green salad. Try the Yogurt Cheese (page 93) as a low-calorie alternative to the sinfully rich *mascarpone*, or substitute regular cream cheese.

Prepare the Basic Pizza Dough, set it aside to rise, and preheat an oven to 500° F. as directed in the basic recipe. If using purchased dough or prebaked crusts, set aside.

Brush a pizza screen or a ventilated pizza pan with vegetable oil or dust a pizza peel with cornmeal; set aside. On a floured surface, roll out the dough and shape it as directed in the basic recipe. Place the crust on the prepared screen, pan, or peel.

Prick the raw dough all over with the tines of a fork and brush it or the prebaked crusts all over with walnut oil or olive oil. Transfer the crust to the preheated oven and bake until the homemade crust begins to brown, 5 to 7 minutes, or until the prebaked crust is warm, about 4 minutes. Remove from the oven to a work surface.

Spread the crust with the *mascarpone* cheese and distribute the nuts over the cheese. Sprinkle with 1 cup of the Parmesan cheese and salt and pepper to taste, and drizzle evenly with walnut oil or olive oil. Return to the oven and bake until the cheese is hot but not completely melted, 4 to 5 minutes longer. Remove from the oven to a cutting tray or board and lightly brush the edges of the crust with walnut oil or olive oil. Sprinkle with the remaining 1 cup Parmesan cheese and garnish with the flowers (if used). Slice and serve immediately.

Makes 4 to 6 main-course servings, or 8 to 10 appetizer servings.

Basic Pizza Dough (page 12), or about
    2 pounds purchased dough, or
    2 large or 4 to 6 individual-sized
    prebaked crusts
Vegetable oil for brushing, if using a
    pizza screen or pizza pan
Cornmeal for dusting, if using a pizza peel
Walnut oil or olive oil, preferably extra-
    virgin, for brushing crust and
    drizzling on top
1 pound *mascarpone* cheese (Italian
    cream cheese), at room temperature
3 cups coarsely chopped walnuts or pecans
2 cups freshly grated Parmesan cheese
    (about 8 ounces), preferably
    Parmigiano-Reggiano
Salt
Freshly ground black pepper
Pesticide-free nontoxic flowers such as
    borage, impatiens, or viola for
    garnish (optional)

Banana Satay Pizza

Basic Pizza Dough (page 12), or about
    2 pounds purchased dough

PEANUT SAUCE
⅔ cup smooth peanut butter
1½ cups homemade or unsweetened
    canned coconut milk
¼ cup vegetable stock, preferably
    homemade
¼ cup heavy (whipping) cream
¼ cup freshly squeezed lemon juice
2 tablespoons soy sauce
2 tablespoons brown sugar or molasses
1 teaspoon grated fresh ginger
2 teaspoons minced or pressed garlic
Ground cayenne pepper

Vegetable oil for brushing, if using a
    pizza screen or pizza pan
Cornmeal for dusting, if using a pizza peel
Canola oil or other high-quality vegetable
    oil for brushing crust
6 ripe yet firm bananas
About 3 tablespoons unsalted butter,
    melted
Chopped roasted peanuts for garnish
Grated lime zest for garnish

Creamy banana is a perfect foil for the spicy peanut sauce of Southeast Asia.

Prepare the Basic Pizza Dough, set it aside to rise, and preheat an oven to 500° F. as directed in the basic recipe. If using purchased dough, set aside.

To make the peanut sauce, in a saucepan, combine the peanut butter, coconut milk, stock, cream, lemon juice, soy sauce, brown sugar or molasses, ginger, garlic, and cayenne pepper to taste. Place over medium heat and cook, stirring constantly, until the sauce is as thick as a cheese sauce, about 15 minutes. Reserve. (This mixture can also be made up to 24 hours ahead, covered, and refrigerated. Return to room temperature before using.)

Brush a pizza screen or a ventilated pizza pan with vegetable oil or dust a pizza peel with cornmeal; set aside. On a floured surface, roll out the dough and shape it as directed in the basic recipe. Place the crust on the prepared screen, pan, or peel.

Brush the dough all over with canola oil or other vegetable oil, then top with the peanut sauce, leaving a ½-inch border around the edges. Slice the bananas lengthwise or into rounds and distribute them over the sauce. Brush the banana slices with the melted butter.

Transfer the pie to the preheated oven and bake until the crust is crisp, 10 to 15 minutes. Remove from the oven to a cutting tray or board and lightly brush the edges of the crust with canola oil or other vegetable oil. Sprinkle with the peanuts and lime zest. Slice and serve immediately.

Makes 4 to 6 main-course servings, or 8 to 10 appetizer servings.

Fresh Figs, Blue Cheese, and Honey Pizza Dolce

Basic Pizza Dough (page 12), preferably
    Sweet Variation, or about 2 pounds
    purchased dough
Vegetable oil for brushing, if using a
    pizza screen or pizza pan
Cornmeal for dusting, if using a pizza peel
Walnut oil or olive oil, preferably extra-
    virgin, for brushing crust
3 cups crumbled creamy blue cheese such
    as Gorgonzola or Cambozola (about
    15 ounces)
About 20 fresh figs, halved lengthwise
High-quality honey for drizzling
About 1 cup Sweet Crunchy Nuts (see
    my book *Salads* for a recipe) or
    toasted walnuts
Fresh fig leaves (optional)

The idea for this recipe came from a delectable combination of triple-creme blue cheese spread on walnut bread and drizzled with honey served by my Napa Valley neighbor and noted food authority Antonia Allegra. I've topped the pizza with walnuts, but you could add chopped nuts to the dough instead to come closer to Antonia's memorable bread. During fig season, I've enjoyed this pizza as an appetizer, dessert, and snack.

Prepare the Basic Pizza Dough, set it aside to rise, and preheat an oven to 500° F. as directed in the basic recipe. If using purchased dough, set aside.

Brush a pizza screen or a ventilated pizza pan with vegetable oil or dust a pizza peel with cornmeal; set aside. On a floured surface, roll out the dough and shape it as directed in the basic recipe. Place the crust on the prepared screen, pan, or peel.

Brush the dough all over with walnut oil or olive oil, then top with the cheese, leaving a ½-inch border around the edges. Arrange the figs, cut side up, over the cheese and drizzle with honey to taste.

Transfer the pie to the preheated oven and bake until the crust is crisp and the cheese and toppings are bubbly, 10 to 15 minutes. Remove from the oven to a cutting tray or board and lightly brush the edges of the crust with walnut oil or olive oil. Top with the nuts. Slice, place on fig leaves (if used), and serve immediately.

Makes 8 appetizer, dessert, or snack servings.

Pizza Colada

Formed into *pizzette* just large enough to hold a pineapple ring, these make unusual appetizers or desserts.

Prepare the Basic Pizza Dough, set it aside to rise, and preheat an oven to 500° F. as directed in the basic recipe. If using purchased dough, set aside.

In a food processor fitted with the metal blade or in a blender, combine the cream cheese, coconut, and rum extract and blend until smooth. Set aside.

Brush a pizza screen or a ventilated pizza pan with vegetable oil or dust a pizza peel with cornmeal; set aside. On a floured surface, roll out the dough and shape it as directed in the basic recipe. Place the crust on the prepared screen, pan, or peel.

Prick the dough all over with the tines of a fork and brush it all over with melted butter. Transfer the crust to the preheated oven and bake until the crust begins to brown, 5 to 7 minutes. Remove from the oven to a work surface.

Spread the crust with the cream cheese mixture. Arrange the pineapple rings over the cheese and lightly brush the pineapple with melted butter. Return to the oven and bake until the cheese is hot but not completely melted, 4 to 5 minutes longer. Remove from the oven to a cutting tray or board and lightly brush the edges of the crust with melted butter. Sprinkle with the toasted coconut and garnish with the flowers (if used). Slice and serve immediately.

Makes 8 appetizer, dessert, or snack servings.

Basic Pizza Dough (page 12), preferably Sweet Variation, or about 2 pounds purchased dough
1 pound cream cheese
1 cup grated fresh or sweetened dried coconut
2 teaspoons rum extract
Vegetable oil for brushing, if using a pizza screen or pizza pan
Cornmeal for dusting, if using a pizza peel
Unsalted butter, melted, for brushing crust and pineapple
8 canned pineapple rings, very well drained
Lightly toasted shredded fresh or sweetened dried coconut for garnish
Pesticide-free nontoxic tropical flowers such as orchids for garnish (optional)

Ricotta Calzonetti Dolce

Basic Pizza Dough (page 12), Sweet
    Variation, or about 2 pounds
    purchased dough
2 cups well-drained high-quality ricotta
    cheese (about 1 pound)
½ cup all-purpose flour
6 tablespoons sugar
4 ounces semisweet chocolate, chopped
3 ounces mixed candied fruit, chopped
3 tablespoons coarsely chopped almonds,
    hazelnuts (filberts), or pistachios
Vegetable oil for brushing, if using a
    pizza screen or pizza pan
Cornmeal for dusting, if using a pizza peel
Unsalted butter, melted, for brushing
    crust
Colored sugar crystals for sprinkling
    (optional)

Inspired by traditional Italian cannoli, these little treats would make an interesting addition to a brunch menu or as a special dessert.

Prepare the Basic Pizza Dough, set it aside to rise, and preheat an oven to 500° F. as directed in the basic recipe. If using purchased dough, set aside.

In a bowl, combine the ricotta cheese, flour, and sugar and mix well. Stir in the chocolate, candied fruit, and nuts. Set aside.

Brush pizza screens or ventilated pizza pans with vegetable oil or dust a pizza peel with cornmeal; set aside. Divide the dough into 18 equal portions. On a floured surface, roll out each piece of the dough and shape it into a round as directed in the basic recipe. Place the rounds on the prepared screens, pans, or peel.

Brush the dough all over with melted butter, then cover half of each dough round with an equal portion of the cheese mixture, leaving a ½-inch border around the edges. Fold the uncovered side over the filling and press the edges of the dough together to seal. Brush the dough all over with melted butter.

Transfer the filled half-moons to the preheated oven and bake until golden brown and puffy, about 15 minutes. Remove from the oven to a work surface and lightly brush with melted butter. Sprinkle with the sugar crystals (if used) and serve immediately.

Makes 6 to 8 dessert or snack servings.

Build-It-Yourself Pizza Party

Basic Pizza Dough (page 12), purchased
    dough, or prebaked individual-sized
    crusts
Vegetable oil for brushing, if using pizza
    screens or pizza pans
Cornmeal for dusting, if using pizza peels
Olive oil, preferably extra-virgin, for
    brushing crust

TOPPINGS
Sliced ripe tomatoes
Sliced red, golden, and/or green sweet
    peppers
Thinly sliced red onion
Sliced green onion
Coarsely chopped garlic
Assorted sliced olives
Olive Paste (*tapénade;* page 54)
Fresh Basil Pesto (page 92)
Slivered or chopped sun-dried tomatoes
    in olive oil
Sliced cooked or marinated artichoke
    hearts
Sautéed or grilled eggplant slices
Tomato Sauce (page 92)
Assorted freshly shredded good-melting
    cheeses such as mozzarella, Cheddar,
    Fontina, smoked Gouda, or Bel Paese
Freshly grated hard cheeses such as
    Parmesan, preferably Parmigiano-
    Reggiano, Asiago, or Pecorino
    Romano
Assorted fresh herbs such as basil leaves,
    minced thyme, chopped flat-leaf
    parsley, chopped cilantro (coriander),
    and chopped rosemary
Salt
Freshly ground black pepper

One of the easiest and most enjoyable parties I stage is held around a kitchen island where piles of ready-baked pizza crusts or balls of fresh dough and a variety of toppings await each guest's originality. If the party is small, I have bowls of risen dough ready for rolling and shaping by each participant. When the crowd is large, I purchase ready-to-top prebaked pizza crusts. There's always a stack of individual-sized pizza screens, bowls of oil, and several brushes.

At the beginning of the pizza-building event, I quickly describe the process of making pizza and then leave everyone to their own creative devices.

A big tossed salad, hearty wine, and a luscious dessert round out the do-ahead menu that allows the host to have as much fun as the guests.

If making your own dough, prepare the Basic Pizza Dough and set it aside to rise. (Each recipe of dough makes enough to serve 4 to 6 people.) Preheat an oven to 500° F. as directed in the basic recipe. If using purchased dough or prebaked crusts, set aside.

On a large work surface, arrange small balls of fresh dough in an oiled bowl or pile prebaked crusts on a platter or in a basket. Position baking screens or peels nearby. Set out bowls of olive oil with brushes alongside. Place each of the selected toppings in a separate bowl, adding labels to identify any ingredients that are not easily identifiable.

Relax and enjoy your party.

Plan on 1 to 2 individual-sized pizzas per person.

Tomato Sauce

Consider making this sauce in quantity during the summer tomato season and freezing it for year-round pizza or pasta topping.

2 tablespoons olive oil
1 cup finely chopped yellow onion
½ cup finely chopped, peeled carrot
½ cup finely chopped celery
2 teaspoons minced or pressed garlic
3 cups peeled, seeded, chopped, and drained ripe or canned tomato
1 tablespoon balsamic vinegar
2 tablespoons minced fresh basil or oregano (optional)
Salt
Freshly ground black pepper

In a saucepan, heat the olive oil over medium heat. Add the onion, carrot, and celery and cook, stirring frequently, until the vegetables are soft but not brown, about 5 minutes. Stir in the garlic, tomato, and vinegar. Increase the heat to high and bring to a boil, then reduce the heat to medium and cook until thickened and most of the liquid evaporates, about 10 minutes. Stir in the herb (if used) about 5 minutes before the sauce is done. Season to taste with salt and pepper.

Transfer the sauce to a food processor fitted with the metal blade or to a blender. Process to a coarse purée. Use immediately, or cover and refrigerate for up to 4 or 5 days.

Makes about 4 cups.

Fresh Tomato Salsa

Spoon onto freshly baked pizza for a sprightly freshness.

2 cups peeled, seeded, chopped, and drained ripe tomato
1 cup finely chopped yellow onion
2 teaspoons minced garlic
2 tablespoons minced fresh hot chile, or to taste
½ cup minced fresh cilantro (coriander)
2 teaspoons freshly squeezed lime juice
Salt

In a bowl, combine all the ingredients, including salt to taste, and mix well. Cover and let stand for at least 1 hour or refrigerate for up to 6 hours.

Makes about 3 cups.

Fresh Basil Pesto

Although pesto is now frequently made from cilantro, parsley, spinach, mint, or a mixture of such greens, and combined with pecans, walnuts, or other nuts, here is the original Italian version.

2 cups firmly packed fresh basil leaves, rinsed and well dried
¼ cup pine nuts
1 tablespoon coarsely chopped garlic
¾ cup freshly grated Parmesan cheese (about 3 ounces), preferably Parmigiano-Reggiano, or a blend of Parmesan and Romano cheeses
½ cup olive oil, preferably extra-virgin
Additional olive oil for storing (optional)

Combine the basil, pine nuts, and garlic in a food processor fitted with the metal blade or in a blender. Purée until smooth. Add the cheese and process to blend. With the motor running, slowly add the oil, continuing to process until well mixed.

Use immediately, or transfer to a container, cover with a thin layer of olive oil to keep the sauce from darkening, and refrigerate for up to 3 days.

Makes about 2 cups.

Red Chile Sauce

Try this as a zesty alternative to your regular pizza sauce.

12 dried whole *ancho, pasilla*, or other dried hot chiles, one kind or a mixture
2 tablespoons olive oil
1 cup chopped yellow onion
2 tablespoons chopped garlic
1 teaspoon dried whole-leaf oregano
½ cup peeled, seeded, chopped, and well-drained ripe or canned tomato
2 cups vegetable stock, preferably homemade
Salt

Preheat an oven to 400° F.

Rinse the chiles under cold running water to remove dust. Shake off excess water and lay the chiles on a baking sheet. Roast in the oven, turning, until lightly toasted on all sides, about 4 minutes; do not burn. Remove from the oven and let cool until they can be handled. Discard the stems, split the chiles open lengthwise, and discard the seeds and membranes, if desired.

In a saucepan over medium-high heat, warm the oil. Add the onion and sauté until soft, about 5 minutes. Stir in the garlic and oregano and sauté for 1 minute longer. Add the reserved chiles, the tomato, and stock. Bring to a boil over high heat, reduce the heat to low, cover, and simmer until the chiles are very tender, about 30 minutes.

Transfer the chile mixture to a food processor fitted with the metal blade or a blender. Purée until smooth. Season to taste with salt.

Using the back of a wooden spoon, rub the purée through a fine-mesh sieve into a clean saucepan. Place over medium heat and cook until slightly thickened, about 10 minutes. If using as an accompaniment, reheat just before serving.

Makes about 2 cups.

Yogurt Cheese

Here is a low-fat substitute for richer cheeses. As with cream cheese, it melts very easily, thus the pizza crust should be partially baked before spreading the cheese onto it.

Once the cheese is made, you may flavor it to taste with minced fresh herbs, cracked black pepper, or minced garlic; or omit the salt and sweeten to taste with sugar or honey.

4 cups plain low-fat yogurt
Salt

Place the yogurt in a cone-type coffee filter with paper liner or in a sieve lined with several layers of cheesecloth. Cover the top with plastic wrap and place over a bowl to drain for about 12 hours.

Discard the whey and use the cheese plain or season as suggested in the recipe introduction. Cover and refrigerate for up to 1 week.

Makes about 2 cups.

Roasted Sweet Peppers or Chiles

Roasting allows you to peel off the tough skin from sweet peppers and hot chiles. It also brings out the sweetness of ripe red, orange, or golden peppers. Tossed in a little olive oil, roasted sweet peppers are delicious on their own as a pizza topping. Or you can cut sweet peppers or chiles into slices or other shapes and use them as colorful additions to mixtures for topping pizzas or as garnishes.

Sweet peppers or chiles

Place the peppers or chiles over a charcoal fire, directly over a gas flame, or under a preheated broiler. Roast, turning several times, until the skin is charred all over. The timing will depend upon the intensity and proximity of the heat. Transfer the peppers or chiles to a paper bag, loosely close the bag, and let stand for about 10 minutes.

Using your fingertips, rub away the charred skin from the peppers. Cut the peppers in half, seed, and remove the membranes. Slice or cut as desired or as directed in individual recipes.

RECIPE INDEX

INDEX TO VEGETARIAN PIZZAS IN OTHER JAMES McNAIR BOOKS

ACKNOWLEDGMENTS

Recipes were tested by:

John Carr
Martha Casselman
Chris Cook
Naila Gallagher
Carol Gallagher
Mark Gullikson
Gail High
Marian May
Debbie Matsumoto
Maile Moore
Sandra Moore
Kristi Spence

To Chronicle Books for the idea for this book and for the continued good work in publishing and promoting my series of cookbooks.

To Sharon Silva for her silvery way with words.

To Cleve Gallat at CTA Graphics for making the design and typography so easy.

To my family and friends who help me in so many ways. Special thanks on this book to John Carr, Martha and Devereux McNair, John Richardson, and Felix Wiench.

To Beauregard Ezekiel Valentine, Joshua J. Chew, Michael T. Wigglebutt, Dweasel Pickle, Miss Vivien Fleigh, and Miss Olivia de Puss Puss for their companionship and for eagerly lapping up all traces of leftover pizza.

To Andrew Moore for his creative ideas for new pizza; his energetic assistance in the office, kitchen, and photo studio; and for taking such great care of me both professionally and personally.